MW01688748

Effective Intercession for Ourselves:
"Power Tools" for Prayer (Part Two)

August 20th 2024

Michelle,

This book has blessed my life and I pray it bless yours! Praying Gods goodness, favor, and blessing!

Love & Appreciate You

Em

# Effective Intercession for Ourselves: "Power Tools" for Prayer (Part Two)

Eric A. Welter

Abound in Hope PRESS

www.aboundinhope.org/press

First Printing: 2024

ISBN 978-1-7344928-2-8

Abound in Hope Press
P.O. Box 1502
Leesburg, Virginia 20177
www.aboundinhope.org/press

Photo Credit: Sarah Sharaf-Eldien, 11:44 Studios.

# Dedication

To St. John the Evangelist, whose inspired writing delivered my father from the fear of death.

# Contents

# Acknowledgements

I give thanks to the Holy Spirit for the inspiration and strength to write this book. Anything good that comes from this book is from You!

I am grateful to my wife Kimberley for her help and encouragement with this book. She reviewed multiple drafts and provided constructive criticism and guidance that made the book better. I am also grateful for her prayers and support not only for this book but in our life together.

I also want to thank those who have given me feedback and encouragement on my first book and other writings. My brother in Christ and physical trainer Eddie M., who finds inspiration in my writing and shares it with others. John B. and his now deceased wife Joanne, who both have given me words of encouragement and support to continue my writing. Ted F., who always has time for a quick note to comment on a new Substack post and encourage me. My Substack subscribers, such as Kevin K., who like my posts and make positive comments. All of this input and encouragement motivates me to keep writing.

Thank you as well to all those who have prayed for me and the writing of this book. I have asked for prayers from many people, including our weekly prayer group and my friends at the Men's Group at St. John the Apostle. This one has definitely been a team effort!

Finally, I want to thank my spiritual mentor, close friend and brother in Christ, Rev. Bro. Augustine Momoh, OP. Thank you for your constant prayers, spiritual guidance and encouragement. Most of all, thank you for your friendship to me and my family. What I have learned from you over the last twenty-four years has been an inspiration and significant influence on this book.

May God bless all who have impacted the writing and production of this book in Jesus' Name. Amen.

# Preface

Looking back on the first *Power Tools* book and how people have received it, I have come to a deeper appreciation of the work of the Holy Spirit. The Holy Spirit not only provided inspiration on topics and scriptural references for the various power tools themselves, but also brought to mind concepts and lessons learned over the years on the spiritual life. My desire in writing the book was to synthesize a great deal of information and life experiences into a smaller package for people to read and (hopefully) benefit fRomans It was ultimately the Holy Spirit, however, who chose to touch people through the words on the page and minister to them.

It seemed like a natural sequel to turn from intercession for others to intercession for ourselves. The start of this second *Power Tools* book flowed quickly off the pen with ideas and inspiration from the Holy Spirit. Each power tool came in order, one after the other. Within a relatively short period of time, I had the framework of the book written. That was in 2020.

More than three years have now gone by. I have worked and re-worked the book during that time. I have encountered long periods of writer's block. There have been periods of spiritual warfare against the book. I set aside the book and focused on my shorter newsletter style articles for a time.[1] Each time I returned and picked up the book, it seemed unfinished. I was unsettled in my spirit.

This year, I increased my requests for the prayers of others to help me cross the finish line. With this prayer support, I finally realized that what was missing from the book was a thread of more practical advice to people about how to implement the power tools in their lives. I was able to add some examples from my life and recommendations for putting different power tools into practice in a more concrete and practical way.

My sincere desire for those who read this book is that the Holy Spirit would teach and minister to you through it. Life is challenging and prayer is a battle. If you only take away one nugget from this book that gives you encouragement and hope to press forward, then I will be grateful that the Holy Spirit has chosen to work through my writing and touch you.

May this book bless you, minister to you and inspire you in your prayers for yourself. God loves you!

---

[1] My writings can be found at https://aboundinhope.substack.com.

# Introduction

Achieving holiness is a life-long process. In God's loving providence, each of us has been given certain obstacles to overcome (or to persevere through out of love for Him) as part of that process.

We have physical, emotional and spiritual ailments. Some are ancestral (inherited). Others we have acquired by sin. Others we have by no fault of our own, perhaps even from the malice of others. We need healing, but we also need deliverance from spiritual bondage. Thanks be to God, our Lord and Saviour Jesus Christ came to destroy the works of the devil![2] The Lord is our healer.[3]

In this book, I propose twelve Scriptural "power tools" for consideration. These twelve power tools can be part of your spiritual arsenal as you pray for yourself. The Holy Spirit may reveal more of them to you in prayer! My hope is that the thoughts in this book would be a starting point for your prayer and reflection, leading you closer to God.

Jesus never said that life would be easy for those who follow Him. Rather, He promised us a cross. Indeed, "prayer is a battle. Against whom? Against ourselves and against the wiles of the tempter who does all he can to turn

---

[2] 1 John 3:8.

[3] Exodus 15:26.

man away from prayer, away from union with God."[4] Prayer is a battle for our sanctification and ultimately our eternal salvation.[5]

Silent prayer and meditation are an important and necessary part of the spiritual life as a Christian. There are parts of the journey, however, that are marked by more difficult challenges and spiritual warfare. The battle can be intense. A more radical form of prayer is often required to defeat our enemies. The power tools in this book will be helpful arrows in your quiver as you battle sin, self and Satan. Have great confidence in God! "The Lord is a man of war."[6]

What should be our focus and disposition as we pray for ourselves? This passage from the Scriptures gives us a clue:

> *Say also: "Deliver us, O God of our salvation, and gather and save us from among the nations, that we may give thanks to thy holy name and glory in thy praise." (1 Chronicles 16:35, RSV-CE).*

We see here that deliverance is not simply for our own sake, but rather that we would thank and praise God for it. **The answered prayers are for the glory of**

---

[4] *Catechism of the Catholic Church* ("CCC") § 2725.

[5] *See* Romans 6:19, 22.

[6] Exodus 15:3, RSV-CE.

**Almighty God.**[7] Keep this in mind as you explore the power tools and go deeper in prayer.

Finally, when you are healed and set free from bondage by the Lord, do not be like the nine lepers who did not return to give Jesus thanks. Be like the one who, "when he saw that he was healed, turned back, praising God with a loud voice; and he fell at Jesus' feet, giving him thanks."[8]

My prayer for you as you read this book are the anointed words of Psalm 20:

> *The Lord answer you in the day of trouble! The name of the God of Jacob protect you! May he send you help from the sanctuary, and give you support from Zion! May he remember all your offerings, and regard with favor your burnt sacrifices! May he grant you your heart's desire, and fulfil all your plans! May we shout for joy over your victory, and in the name of our God set up our banners! May the Lord fulfil all your petitions! (Psalm 20:1-5, RSV-CE).*

I lift my hands and pray this over you today in the mighty Name of Jesus! Amen!

---

[7] *Compare* Psalm 106:8.

[8] Luke 17:15-16, RSV-CE.

# The Power of Truth

## Promise in God's Word

*Strive even to death for the truth and the Lord God will fight for you. (Sirach 4:28, RSV-CE).*

## Reflection

There is a moment of great drama during the interrogation of Jesus by Pontius Pilate (the governor of the Roman province of Judaea) leading up to the crucifixion of Jesus. Pilate asked Jesus if He was the King of the Jews. Jesus replied that his kingship was not of this world. Pilate followed up with, "Your own nation and the chief priests have handed you over to me; what have you done?" Jesus boldly responded to Pilate by proclaiming:

> *"You say that I am a king. For this I was born, and for this I have come into the world, to bear witness to the truth. Every one who is of the truth hears my voice." (John 18:37, RSV-CE).*[9]

In response, Pilate asked the famous question:

*"What is truth?" (John 18:38, RSV-CE).*

That is the question we need to ponder — what is truth?

[9] *See also* John 3:32, 8:14, 47; 1 John 4:6.

I encountered the hard reality of "truth" as a child. The walk home from elementary school took me past the neighborhood convenience store. My mother had strictly enjoined me not to stop at the store on the way home. Although I do not remember what possessed me to disobey and stop one day, I did go into the store. I went home right after.

As a child, I did not realize that my six-foot tall mother could see the front door to the convenience store over the backyard fence. When I did not come home on time, she watched her son exit the store from our living room. When I returned home, I was confronted with the question: "Did you stop at the store on the way home?"

I made the wrong choice. "No," I responded.

Well, you would have thought the world was coming to an end. I was informed that we did not have liars in our family, that I was lying to her, and that I was banished from the family. I was sent to my room.

As the story goes, after spending the day in my room, including eating dinner alone there, I decided that I wanted to be part of the family again. I repented of my lying and was re-admitted to participation in the household.

The hard lesson stuck with me for life. Truth is not a negotiable principle for me. The quickest way to lose my respect is to exhibit dishonesty.

Why is truth so important when we pray for ourselves? The primary reason is that the knowing misrepresentation of the truth is an offense against God. The eighth commandment states that "You shall not bear false witness against your neighbor."[10] It "forbids misrepresenting the truth in our relations with others."[11] An offense committed against the truth is serious and requires reparation.[12] If we are pursuing holiness, it is critical that we avoid offenses against the truth.[13]

The Bible is clear that God does not hear the prayers of evildoers.[14] Do you want to be a child of the devil, the father of lies? Or do you want to be a child of God, and be in a posture to be praying to your Heavenly Father for assistance?

Truth is also a critical piece of our spiritual armor. St. Paul teaches in Chapter 6 of the Letter to the Ephesians that we are in a battle with spiritual powers and principalities, world rulers of this present darkness and spiritual hosts of wickedness.[15] He exhorts us to put on

---

[10] Exodus 20:16.

[11] CCC § 2464.

[12] CCC § 2509.

[13] CCC §§ 2475-87.

[14] *See* Proverbs 15:29, 28:9; Ps. 66:18; Isaiah 59:2; John 9:31; 1 Peter 3:12.

[15] Ephesians 6:12.

the whole armor of God for this battle and explains each piece of the armor. The first piece of armor listed is that of truth.

> *Therefore take the whole armor of God, that you may be able to withstand in the evil day, and having done all, to stand. Stand therefore, having girded your loins with truth. (Ephesians 6:13-14, RSV-CE).*

In the ancient world, the command to gird up one's loins was the first command given before gearing up for battle. Girding up the tunic ensured there was no impediment to the soldier running. Girding ourselves spiritually with truth also guards our strength.[16]

Girding the loins also marked the start of the journey to the Promised Land. God commanded the Israelites to gird their loins before they ate the Passover supper.[17] This was the first step on their journey of deliverance from Egypt.

Jesus likewise uses this image when He tells us to be prepared spiritually for His coming. He instructs us: "Let your loins be girded and your lamps burning."[18] God the

---

[16] St. John Chrysostom on Ephesians, Ch. 6 (Patristic Bible Commentary online) (https://sites.google.com/site/aquinasstudybible/home).

[17] Exodus 12:11.

[18] Luke 12:35, RSV-CE.

Father likewise admonishes us to get ready as we open ourselves to the truth: "Gird up your loins like a man."[19]

Jesus alludes to the need for us to actively seek truth in the Sermon on the Mount. He tells us:

> *"Blessed are those who hunger and thirst for righteousness, for they shall be satisfied." (Matthew 5:6, RSV-CE).*

This Beatitude speaks to "[t]hose who yearn to live rightly according to the will of God."[20] It is only by living in truth that we can become aligned with God's will.[21] In other words, we should hunger "spiritually, with an earnest desire of being just and holy."[22]

This again brings us to the question that we started this chapter with – what is truth?

The starting point in answering this question is to understand that the truth is a person. **Jesus is the Truth.** He is the one that told us this.

---

[19] Job 38:3, RSV-CE.

[20] *Ignatius Catholic Study Bible (New Testament),* note on Matthew 5:6 (2d Ed.) (Ignatius Press 2010).

[21] Eric A. Welter, *Effective Intercession for Our Loved Ones,* at 19-23 (power of righteousness) (Abound in Hope Press 2020).

[22] Haydock, George Leo, *George Haydock's Catholic Bible Commentary,* Commentary on Matthew 5 (1859) (online at http://tinyurl.com/yts3pj5r).

*I am the way, the truth, and the life. No one comes to the Father, but by me. (John 14:6, RSV-CE).*

Indeed, **"God's very being is Truth and Love."**[23] God the Father revealed His Truth to us by sending Jesus. Ponder for a moment what a great gift that is to us!

*And we know that the Son of God has come and has given us understanding, to know him who is true; and we are in him who is true, in his Son Jesus Christ. This is the true God and eternal life. (1 John 5:20-21, RSV-CE).*

We currently live, however, in a time of mass deception and darkness. It is quite accurate to say that we currently live under a dictatorship of moral relativism.[24] "Your truth is not my truth" is one way this relativism is expressed today, as people reject traditional Judeo-Christian moral teachings and justify sin. Yet, moral relativism is not truth and it is not Christian.

False doctrines are widely accepted by both Christians and non-Christians. New Age and occultic spirituality have infected the spiritual lives of many

---

[23] CCC § 231, *see* CCC §§ 215-221.

[24] *Homily of Card. Joseph Ratzinger,* Dean of the College of Cardinals, Vatican Basilica, Monday 18 April 2005 (available as of July 24, 2020, at: https://tinyurl.com/2p8hr9c9).

people, even unknowingly at times.[25] Demons are like spiritual bacteria[26] — do you have a spiritual infection?

When we set out to learn the truth, we should have confidence that God wants us to find the truth. The Word of God promises us that God "desires all men to be saved and to come to the knowledge of the truth."[27] It is God's desire that you come to know the truth. So where do you start? What is our spiritual penicillin? Have courage and start by putting on the mind of Christ![28]

To come to learn the truth, we must call on the Holy Spirit. Jesus sent the Holy Spirit for this very purpose — to help us come to know the truth:

> *When the Spirit of truth comes, he will guide you into all the truth. (John 16:13, RSV-CE).*

We should examine ourselves and reflect on how we can "strive even to death for the truth" in our lives. Here are some starting points for consideration as you reflect on whether you are a person of the truth:

---

[25] Hosea 4:6, RSV-CE ("My people are destroyed for lack of knowledge").

[26] Rev. Bro. Augustine Momoh, O.P., *Christian Faith and Supernatural Reality*, at 18 (Wellness for Humanity Ministry 2018).

[27] 1 Timothy 2:4, RSV-CE.

[28] 1 Corinthians 2:16.

- St. Augustine defines a lie as "speaking a falsehood with the intention of deceiving."[29] Do I strive to be honest or do I tell lies?
- Am I a person of my word? When I say that I will do something, can people rely on me?[30]
- Have I been guilty of rash judgment (assuming as true, without sufficient basis, the moral fault of another)?
- Have I been guilty of detraction (disclosing another's faults and failings to persons who did not know them without a valid reason)?
- Have I been guilty of calumny (harming the reputation of others by false statements)?
- Do I gossip or back-bite?

As we work to become people of the truth, the Scriptural promise of this power tool will begin to manifest itself in our lives. God will fight for you. Jesus promised us that the truth would set us free.[31]

Psalm 53 (Douay-Rheims)[32] is a great prayer that we can use in our spiritual arsenal as we pray for ourselves. We can pray this Psalm in times of trouble, spiritual

---

29 CCC § 2482 (*citing* St. Augustine, *De mendacio* 4, 5: PL 40: 491).

30 Matthew 5:37 ("Let what you say be simply 'Yes' or 'No;' anything more than this comes from evil.").

31 John 8:31-32.

32 Other Bible versions/translations have this as Psalm 54, and the translation of verse 7 is different.

distress or persecution. Tradition holds that King David composed this Psalm after God rescued him from Saul by sending the Philistines into the land, distracting Saul from his pursuit of David.[33] When you pray this Psalm, pray it out loud and with vigor!

> *Save me, O God, by thy name, and judge me in thy strength. O God, hear my prayer: give ear to the words of my mouth. For strangers have risen up against me; and the mighty have sought after my soul: and they have not set God before their eyes. For behold God is my helper: and the Lord is the protector of my soul. Turn back the evils upon my enemies; and* ***cut them off in thy truth****.*[34] *I will freely sacrifice to thee, and will give praise, O God, to thy name: because it is good: For thou hast delivered me out of all trouble: and my eye hath looked down upon my enemies. (Psalm 53:3-9, Douay-Rheims).*[35]

---

[33] 1 Samuel 23:19-28 (RSV-CE); 1 Kings 23:19-28 (Douay-Rheims).

[34] Verse 7 in the Latin Vulgate Bible states "*Averte mala inimicis meis; et in veritate tua disperde illos.*" The Latin word "*disperdo*" has a much stronger meaning than the translation above—it means "to destroy" or "to ruin utterly." The prayer asks God to destroy our enemies to fulfill His promises (i.e., His truth). *See The Holy Bible According to the Douay and Rheimish Versions With the Complete Notes of the Rev. Geo. Leo Haydock,* note on Ps. 53:7 at p. 728 (Edward Dunigan and Brother, New York 1859) (reprinted by Catholic Treasures (1992)).

[35] Verses 6-7 compose the *Introit* in the Traditional Latin Mass for the Ninth Sunday After Pentecost.

Pray with me right now for the Holy Spirit to come into your life and lead you into all the truth! "[P]ray to the Most High that he may direct your way in truth."[36]

Come Holy Spirit, Spirit of truth; come into my life, come into my soul, come into my body, enlighten my mind; remove every blockage to the truth from my life, mind, body and spirit in the Name of Jesus! Amen.

---

[36] Sirach 37:15, RSV-CE.

## Additional Resources

Related Scriptures:

Sir. 20:24-26; Ps. 101:7, 145:18; Isaiah 45:19; Luke 8:15; John 4:23-24, 8:46-47; 17:3, 18:37-38; 1 Cor. 5:7-8; 2 Thes. 2:9-12; Ephesians 4:15.

Songs:

*"Voice of Truth"* — Song by Casting Crowns from the album *Casting Crowns* (Released 2003).
(A YouTube video of the song can be watched here: https://tinyurl.com/yxme7cg9.)

*"Who You Say I Am"* — Song by Hillsong Worship from the album *There is More* (Released 2018).
(A YouTube video of the song can be watched here: https://tinyurl.com/y3mlw4w7.)

*"Here's My Heart"* — Song by Casting Crowns (Live music video 2015).
(A YouTube video of the song can be watched here: https://tinyurl.com/yxdb5tac.)

Prayer:

> *Grant, O Lord, unto Thy people grace to withstand the temptations of the devil, and with pure minds to follow Thee, the only God.*

*Collect* (Prayer) for the 17th Sunday after Pentecost (Roman Catholic Traditional Latin Mass (Extraordinary Form)).

Additional Reading:

*Live Not By Lies,* Alexander Solzhenitsyn (Feb. 12, 1974) (available as of Feb. 15, 2022, at https://www.solzhenitsyncenter.org/live-not-by-lies).

*Veritatis splendor,* Encyclical letter of John Paul II (Aug. 6, 1993) (available as of November 3, 2021 at https://tinyurl.com/yg8cxpy4).

Additional Points for Reflection:

Journey to the Promised Land: Exodus 12:11.

Armor of God: Ephesians 6:14.

Beatitude: Matthew 5:6.

Gift of the Holy Spirit: Wisdom.

# The Power of Integrity

## Promise in God's Word

*He who walks in integrity will be delivered. (Proverbs 28:18, RSV-CE).*

## Reflection

Jesus told the apostles at the end of the Last Supper, "The ruler of this world is coming. He has no power over me."[37] One truth that each of us must confront at some point in our life is that we may not be able to say the same thing. Can you honestly say that the enemy has no power over you?

The kind of power we are talking about here is spiritual bondage. Are you troubled with recurring sin, especially a serious one? Are you bound by addiction to alcohol, drugs or pornography? Are you spiritually attacked by fear, depression or anxiety? Are you tormented with thoughts of suicide? Are you facing even worse spiritual problems? What is the solution?

Only Jesus can deliver and heal you. This power tool from the Word of God, which promises deliverance, is a starting point on the path to freedom.

---

[37] John 14:30, RSV-CE. Another translation reads "the prince of this world cometh, and in me he hath not any thing." (John 14:30, Douay-Rheims).

The *Oxford English Dictionary* defines "integrity" as "The quality of being honest and having strong moral principles." By definition, this naturally follows and flows from the power tool of truth. **Living in the truth and walking in integrity are the foundation for self-deliverance.**

I witnessed this biblical promise unfold in the life of my father. My father was a cradle Catholic who attended Mass every Sunday. Professionally, he was an attorney. After he passed away, I heard testimonies about my father having been a man of unwavering integrity. This had also been my experience knowing him.

The last six years of my father's life were spent battling colon cancer. I visited him in Minnesota shortly after he was finally sent home by the doctors, having been told that there were no more treatments available to battle the spreading cancer. We sat down and talked. He confessed that he was afraid to die because he was afraid of God. He had been raised during a generation in the Church that was focused on rules instead of relationship. This put him in a position of fear in relation to God. The Holy Spirit provided me with words of direction and encouragement for my father – I told him to read the first letter of St. John.

After returning to Virginia from the visit, my mother called. "What did you say to your father? He asked me to make a copy of the first letter of St. John from the Bible. He never reads the Bible."

Shortly after that, I was able to be present when my father passed away. I know that he had been delivered of his fear. He died peacefully. I see now that God honored the promise He made in His Word: *He who walks in integrity will be delivered.*

As with truth, integrity is part of our spiritual armor. St. Paul encourages us to "put on the breastplate of righteousness" as part of the armor of God.[38] To St. Paul, the breastplate of righteousness "means a life of universal virtue,"[39] i.e., integrity. St. Thomas Aquinas teaches that "justice is referred to as a breastplate because it covers all the virtues."[40] This is also consistent with living a life of integrity.

When we think about a breastplate, we realize what an important part of the armor it is — it protects the heart.[41] "In biblical terms, the heart is the hidden center of the person where one's thoughts, words, actions, and emotions are said to originate."[42] We need this protection

---

[38] Ephesians 6:14, RSV-CE.

[39] *St. John Chrysostom on Ephesians,* Chapter 6, *supra; see also Effective Intercession for Our Loved Ones*, at 19-22 (power tool of righteousness).

[40] St. Thomas Aquinas, *Commentary on Saint Paul's Epistle to the Ephesians* (Magi Books 1966) (a copy can be found online as of Sept. 4, 2020, here: https://isidore.co/aquinas/SSEphesianshtm).

[41] Mother Nadine Brown, *God's Armor,* at 90 (Intercessors of the Lamb 1998).

[42] *Ignatius Bible,* note on Matthew 5:8, at 14.

of our heart by the breastplate because of the biblical promise given the pure of heart. The pure in heart here are "those who act with integrity and serve the Lord unselfishly."[43]

> *Blessed are the pure in heart, for they shall see God. (Matthew 5:8, RSV-CE).*

As we strive for purity of heart, living a life of virtue and integrity, the eyes of our spirit will be opened to see Almighty God. In His presence, we are loved and protected.

> *By this I know that thou art pleased with me, in that my enemy has not triumphed over me. But thou hast upheld me because of my integrity, and set me in thy presence for ever. (Psalm 41:11-12, RSV-CE).*

The life of integrity is also one governed by the law of God. God revealed to the Israelites the Ten Commandments[44] and the Divine Law.[45] If you have not read these chapters in the Old Testament, you should. As you prayerfully read the commands given to Moses for God's chosen people, ponder what the perspective of the never-changing God is on these issues today. "The moral precepts [of the law] were to continue, and to be complied

---

[43] *Ignatius Bible,* note on Matthew 5:8, at 14.

[44] Exodus 20.

[45] Genesis 21-23.

with, even with greater perfection."[46] Jesus said that He did not come to abolish the law, but to perfect it.[47]

As we strive for integrity, we should imitate Jesus. Jesus is the perfect model of integrity. He is Truth itself, and is never-changing.

> *Jesus Christ is the same yesterday and today and for ever. (Hebrews 13:8, RSV-CE).*

Although we strive to imitate Jesus, we recognize that He is Divine and without sin. Where can we look for real people who are models of integrity?

The Old Testament gives us many examples of ordinary people who lived with integrity. Joseph, sold into slavery in Egypt, resisted the adulterous overtures of his master's wife[48] and eventually was made steward over the nation of Egypt.[49] Daniel refused to compromise the practice of the Jewish faith, and was spared by God from death in the lion's den.[50] The three young men refused to bow down and worship the golden image of the king, were placed in the fiery furnace and survived under the

---

46 *Haydock Bible,* note on Matthew 5:17.

47 Matthew 5:17.

48 Genesis 39.

49 Genesis 41.

50 Dan. 6.

protection of God's angel.[51] "Eleazor, one of the scribes in high position, a man now advanced in age and noble presence," chose death over eating pork in violation of the Law.[52] He likewise rejected faking compliance by eating acceptable meat to avoid giving a bad example to the young and leading them astray.[53] "So in this way he died, leaving in his death an example of nobility and a memorial of courage, not only to the young but to the great body of his nation."[54]

The Holy Spirit also reveals to us another aspect of integrity in the Old Testament Book of Job. God says to Satan, "Have you considered my servant Job, that there is none like him on the earth, a blameless and upright man, who fears God and turns away from evil?"[55] God places all that Job has in Satan's power and Satan ravages everything. The Holy Spirit then tells us that "[i]n all this Job did not sin or charge God with wrong."[56]

After this, the Lord confronts Satan by saying, "Have you considered my servant Job, that there is none like him on the earth, a blameless and upright man, who fears God

---

[51] Daniel 3.

[52] 2 Maccabees 6:18-20, RSV-CE.

[53] 2 Maccabees 6:21-28.

[54] 2 Maccabees 6:31, RSV-CE.

[55] Job 1:8, RSV-CE.

[56] Job 1:22, RSV-CE.

and turns away from evil? He still holds fast his integrity, although you moved me against him, to destroy him without cause."[57] We see here that one aspect of integrity is not to charge God with wrong when things do not go well for us.

We also see examples of integrity in the New Testament, particularly where the early disciples of Jesus proclaimed the Gospel truth without fear. St. Peter and St. John continued to preach Jesus, despite being ordered not to do so by the Jewish authorities.[58] St. Paul preached the Gospel everywhere he went, despite being lashed five times, beaten with rods three times and stoned once.[59]

Even in our lives, we can think of situations where the integrity of someone has made an impact on us. Our witness of integrity can change lives. In my life, my father Paul was a witness of integrity. Despite challenges and troubles, I never saw him waver in his integrity. This was a powerful example that influenced all aspects of my adult life.

Is there someone in your life who has been a witness of integrity? Have you been an example of integrity to those around you? As you reflect on the biblical examples of integrity, what is the Holy Spirit speaking to your heart

---

[57] Job 2:3, RSV-CE.

[58] Acts 4.

[59] 2 Corinthians 11:24-31.

about how to change your life? Do we need to repent of those times where we may have charged God with wrong when things did not go well for us? Are we serving the Lord unselfishly?

My prayer for you is that you will stand firm in the truth, walking in integrity before God. God will uphold you and deliver you because of your integrity! May the Lord deliver you from every bondage, from every slavery to sin, from every evil and attack of the enemy, and set you in His presence forever, in Jesus' Name! Amen.

## Additional Resources

Related Scriptures:

1 Kings 9:4; 1 Sam. 12:1-5; Job 2:3, 2:9; Ps. 25:21, 26:1, 11, 101:2-3; Proverbs 2:7, 10:9, 11:3, 19:1, 20:7, 28:6; Sir. 7:6; Isaiah 59:17; Titus 2:7.

Songs:

*"Even If"* — Song by Mercy Me from the album *Lifer* (Released 2017).
(A YouTube video of the song can be watched here: https://tinyurl.com/koyouk8.)

*"If We're Honest"* — Song by Francesca Battistelli from the album *If We're Honest* (Released 2014).
(A YouTube video of the song can be watched here: https://tinyurl.com/y5torr8o.)

Prayer:

Psalm 26 (RSV-CE).

Additional Points for Reflection:

Journey to the Promised Land: Exodus Ch. 20.

Armor of God: Ephesians 6:14.

Beatitude: Matthew 5:8.

Gift of the Holy Spirit: Counsel.

# The Power of Patience

## Promise in God's Word

*Thou dost deliver those who wait for thee. (Sirach 51:8, RSV-CE).*

## Reflection

They say patience is a virtue. For most of us, this is a work in progress! We want what we want, now.

We live in a time of advanced technology. In 1965, Gordon E. Moore, the co-founder of Intel, made the observation that the number of transistors on a microchip doubles about every two years, though the cost of computers is halved. "Moore's Law," as it is called, also says that the growth of microprocessors is exponential. Despite predictions to the contrary, as of the writing of this book almost sixty years later, Moore's Law continues to be accurate.

Many of us have experienced this dizzying growth in the power of technology in our lives. In the early 1990s when I started practicing law, the fax machine was new. There was no internet or email. When cell phones were introduced, you had to carry them in a briefcase. First generation internet connections were dial up over telephone lines.[60]

Today, we have broadband internet service over fiber optic cable. Where we used to have to wait for a picture to download over dial-up, now we can stream and watch entire movies. If the Wi-Fi connection is slow today, however, our impatience immediately flares up!

We have developed false expectations as a result of this convenience. One of the biggest false expectations today is that there is a "quick fix" to our spiritual problems. This is not true. There is often not a quick fix to a spiritual problem. As a result, people give up too easily in trying to overcome their spiritual problems.

We must approach our prayers for ourselves — for our healing, deliverance and sanctification — with patience. Some of our spiritual problems are ancestral. They took generations to develop and will not go away in an instant. Some of our spiritual problems are the result of years of sin and iniquity in our life. Likewise, they will not go away in an instant. Patience is required in order to overcome obstacles in the spiritual life.

I now look back on almost thirty years of trying to live a Christian spiritual life and see how God works

---

[60] For those unfamiliar with dial-up internet, you can read about it and watch a short video that includes the infamous dial-up connection sound here: http://tinyurl.com/2heykmsm.

through our patience. The first phase of my return to the faith is instructive.

After I returned to the Church in my late 20s, I had much to learn about the Faith.[61] I attended Mass every Sunday. I went to Benediction at a weekly Holy Hour and became familiar with traditional Catholic hymns. I learned how to pray the rosary. I started reading the Bible and books about the Faith. Even though my prayer life was very basic at this time, I was laying a foundation. I was also vigorously fighting the battle against sin and bad habits.

After several years, I traveled to Omaha, Nebraska to go on a 4-day silent retreat. One significant part of the religious order's charism was to hold silent retreats for individuals and help guide them into mental prayer. They vigorously interceded in prayer for the retreatants.

During the years leading up to the retreat, I had to go to confession frequently because I was battling habitual mortal sin. Quite frankly, it was humiliating and depressing to continually fall over and over again. It was as if I could not control myself, even though I knew it was wrong. I prayed and prayed to be set free. I also had an addiction to chewing tobacco that I absolutely could not

---

[61] I discuss my reversion and return to the Church in the last chapter of this book.

kick. The nicotine addiction happens to run parallel to my habitual mortal sin problem, so I use it to tell the story.

I was introduced to chewing tobacco when I was 14 years old at summer camp. The older boys liked to give the new campers some tobacco and then watch them throw up. I did not throw up – I became addicted. I continued to use tobacco in high school, college and law school. After I was married and started practicing law, I continued to use tobacco. I tried to quit off and on, but it was after we had our son that I became seriously conflicted about continuing to use tobacco. I discovered, however, that I could not quit – it had become a physical and spiritual compulsion. I would try to quit all day at work, and then find myself driving to the store at 9pm to buy another can! When I left to go on my silent retreat in Omaha, I left home without any tobacco, determined to quit.

One day during the retreat, I went to confession. The priest was an exorcist. As I discussed my habitual mortal sin problem, he explained to me that sometimes these compulsive sins can be demonic in origin. He explained that he could say a binding prayer over me, to "bind up" any demons behind the problem and give me an opportunity to grow in prayer and virtue without constantly battling this sin. Even if the problem was not demonic, there was no harm in him saying the prayers. I agreed, and Father prayed over me. The retreat continued.

That evening, with the entire group of brothers and sisters in the religious community, the Mother Superior asked me what I wanted them to pray for when they prayed over me. One specific intention I had was to be able to quit chewing tobacco – to be set free from this addiction. She asked me, "Do you really want to quit?" (I thought this was a silly question.) She explained to me that many people ask them for help to quit smoking, but then start again. She had learned through prayer and experience that the person truly needed to want to quit. In her words, "If God were to answer your prayer and completely take it away, would you be ok with that? Are you ready to quit?" I answered yes, I was ready to quit. They prayed over me. The retreat continued.

The next day, I was taking a long walk around the neighborhood. I saw something hanging from a tree in my path. Impaled on a tree at eye level was a can of Skoal chewing tobacco. Honest!

I went home after the retreat and have never had the urge for tobacco again. That was over 25 years ago. By the way, I did not have to confess the habitual mortal sin ever again. Thank you, Jesus!

Patience is a key weapon in the arsenal of a spiritual warrior. Patience is "the ability to wait, or to continue doing something despite difficulties, or to suffer without complaining or becoming annoyed."[62] We have laid the groundwork for the journey by girding our loins with the truth and putting on integrity as our breastplate. Now, we must add patience to our armor. St. Paul counsels us, as part of the armor of God, to "keep alert with all perseverance."[63] "Our perseverance in prayer must match the relentless persistence of the devil."[64]

The Gospels present us with a story to reflect upon when we are facing the need for patience in our prayers for ourselves, especially when things are not happening as quickly as we might like. There was a woman with a flow of blood for twelve years, who had spent everything she had and suffered under many physicians, but had only gotten worse.[65] She heard reports about Jesus and sought him out. She thought, if only I could touch his garments, I will be made well. Coming up behind him in the crowd, she touched his garment and was healed!

The rest of the story is interesting and worth reading, but the first part is worthy of meditation upon patience. We see the reward here of the woman's patience. Despite having spent everything she had on useless treatments,

---

[62] *Cambridge Dictionary* (available as of August 17, 2020, here: https://dictionary.cambridge.org/us/dictionary/english/patience).

[63] Ephesians 6:18, RSV-CE.

[64] *Ignatius Bible*, note on Ephesians 6:18, at 354.

[65] Mark 5:25-34; Matthew 9:20-22; Luke 8:43-48.

suffering for twelve years, and no one able to heal her,[66] she did not roll over and die. Rather, she sought out Jesus, with a mighty faith that just touching his garment would unleash Divine healing power into her. Jesus acknowledged to her, "Daughter, your faith has made you well."[67] Likewise, I encourage you to have patience with the process. Do not give up!

We see that patience involves peaceful acceptance of suffering.[68] The prophet Baruch prophetically coaches us to endure with patience:

> *My children, endure with patience the wrath that has come upon you from God. Your enemy has overtaken you, but you will soon see their destruction and will tread upon their necks. (Baruch 4:25, RSV-CE).*

The great mystic writer St. John of the Cross also counsels us to have patience in trials:

---

[66] *See* Luke 8:43, RSV-CE.

[67] Mark 5:34, RSV-CE.

[68] *See The Holy Bible According to the Douay and Rheimish Versions With the Complete Notes of the Rev. Geo. Leo Haydock*, note on 1 Thessalonians 1:3 at p. 1558 (Edward Dunigan and Brother, New York 1859) (reprinted by Catholic Treasures (1992)) ("The apostle praises the Thessalonians for the progress they had made in the theological virtues [of faith, hope, and charity], and enumerates the profit they had derived from each. Their faith had produced works; their charity rendered their labour light and easy, and their patience was the fruit of their future hopes, in confidence of which they bore what they had to suffer from their unconverted countrymen. (Estius)").

> *People, then, should live with great patience and constancy in all the tribulations and trials God places on them, whether they be exterior or interior, spiritual or bodily, great or small, and they should accept them all as from God's hand as a good remedy and not flee from them, for they bring health. . . . [T]here is not a trial that does not have a corresponding and considerable reward.*[69]

There are good reasons why God does not always give us complete freedom in an instant. **If God were to drive out our spiritual enemies immediately, would we be prepared to occupy the land that was vacated?**

God told the Israelites as they entered the Promised Land that He "would not drive them [i.e., their enemies] out from before you in one year, lest the land become desolate and the wild beasts multiply against you."[70] Rather, He said, "Little by little I will drive them out before you, until you are increased and possess the land."[71]

This is true in the process of spiritual healing and deliverance. As we cooperate with God and grow in grace and virtue, He drives out the enemy from our territory.

---

[69] *The Collected Words of St. John of the Cross*, at 669 (ICS Publications 1991).

[70] Exodus 23:29, RSV-CE.

[71] Exodus 23:30, RSV-CE.

Through a life of consistent prayer, the Holy Spirit claims the territory that was vacated, creating a stronghold for God. Little by little, God reclaims your body, soul and spirit for Himself and His kingdom.

This is also a promise in the Beatitudes. Jesus said:

> *"Blessed are the meek: for they shall possess the land." (Matthew 5:4, Douay-Rheims).*

This land promised to the meek is "the land of the living, or the kingdom of heaven."[72] This is what we are seeking!

*Webster's American Dictionary of the English Language* (1828) defines meek as "mild of temper; soft; gentle; not easily provoked or irritated; yielding; given to forbearance under injuries." To be meek requires patience, for meekness is the virtue of not responding in anger when wronged.

> *Meekness is a virtue which implies loftiness of soul. . . . And so the servants of God, remaining always quiet and peaceable, though provoked by words or acts, manifest a perfect loftiness of soul superior to all rudeness.*[73]

Note that meekness does not mean weakness. Rather, it means strength under control. The Bible

---

[72] *Haydock Bible*, note on Matthew 5:4; *Ignatius Bible*, note on Matthew 5:4, at 14.

[73] Attributed to St. Thomas Aquinas.

describes Moses as the meekest of all men[74] and yet we see Moses exhibiting great strength of character, faith and patience throughout his ministry. We should also imitate Jesus in meekness.

> *"Take up my yoke upon you, and learn of me, because I am meek, and humble of heart: and you shall find rest to your souls." (Matthew 11:29, RSV-CE).*

As we strive to practice patience in all the circumstances of life, let us continue to have great confidence in Almighty God:

> *There is no difficulty in our lives for which God does not know the solution. From all eternity He has foreseen it and has the remedy for each case, no matter how complicated the situation may be. However, sometimes in difficult circumstances He seems to leave us alone as if the outcome were to depend on us, but He does this only to test us. He wants us to measure our strength against the difficulty – which makes us more aware of our weakness and insufficiency – and He wants us also to exercise our faith and our confidence in Him. The Lord never really abandons us unless we forsake Him first. He only hides Himself and covers His actions with a dark veil. This is the time to believe,*

---

[74] Numbers 12:3.

> *to believe firmly, and to wait with humble patience and complete confidence.*[75]

We must seek the Lord in prayer with great patience. My prayer for you is that you would adopt a consistent daily time for prayer and resolve to be faithful to your commitment. If you do not have a habit of prayer, start with something small—perhaps five minutes a day when you wake up. If you already have daily prayer time, add a daily routine of prayerful reading of Scripture. The important part is to keep doing it!

Once you have entered the battle of prayer, I pray that you will stand firm, patiently and faithfully waiting for God to take back the land. Jesus assures us:

> *In your patience you shall possess your souls. (Luke 21:19, Douay-Rheims).*

[75] *Divine Intimacy—Meditations on the Interior Life for Every Day of the Liturgical Year,* at 351 (Tan Books 1996) (originally published in English in 1964).

## Additional Resources

Related Scriptures:

Exodus 14:13-14; Lam. 3:25; Ps. 37; Sir. 16:13; Luke 8:15; Romans 2:7, 8:25, 9:22; Gal. 5:22-23; Col. 1:11-12, 3:12; Jas. 1:2-4, 5:7.

Songs:

*"While I Wait"* — Song by Lincoln Brewster from the album *God of the Impossible* (Released 2018)
(A YouTube video of the song can be watched here: https://tinyurl.com/y4o53rsl.)

Prayer:

Rosary, Fourth Sorrowful Mystery — Carrying of the Cross (*Luke 23:26-33*) (Fruit of the mystery: patience).

Additional Points for Reflection:

Journey to the Promised Land: Exodus 23:29-30.

Armor of God: Ephesians 6:18.

Beatitude: Matthew 5:5.

Gift of the Holy Spirit: Fortitude.

# The Power of Hope

## Promise in God's Word

*The Lord will help them and deliver them and he will rescue them from the wicked, and save them, because they have hoped in him. (Psalm 36:40, Douay-Rheims).*

## Reflection

What is hope? "Hope is the theological virtue by which we desire the kingdom of heaven and eternal life as our happiness, placing our trust in Christ's promises and relying not on our own strength, but on the help of the grace of the Holy Spirit."[76] "The object of hope is the possession of God and eternal beatitude."[77] Christian hope is focused on heaven and is the springboard for our life of prayer.

Hope bears the fruit of patience. "Hope is practiced through the virtue of patience, which continues to do good even in the face of apparent failure, and through the virtue

[76] CCC § 1817.

[77] *Divine Intimacy,* at 896.

of humility, which accepts God's mystery and trusts Him even at times of darkness."[78]

"[W]e prove that our hope is strong by continuing to hope in spite of adversity and even when God seems to have abandoned us."[79] St. Paul reminds us that hope does not disappoint us:

> *We rejoice in our sufferings, knowing that suffering produces endurance, and endurance produces character, and character produces hope, and hope does not disappoint us, because God's love has been poured into our hearts through the Holy Spirit who has been given to us. (Romans 5:3-5, RSV-CE).*

What should we place our hope in?

First, we should firmly hope that God wants us to become holy and be with Him in heaven. The Bible tells us that God "desires all men to be saved and to come to the knowledge of the truth,"[80] and that it is God's will for us to become holy.[81] Your journey through this book is evidence of this truth!

---

[78] *God is Love (Deus Caritas Est)*, Encyclical Letter of Benedict XVI, ¶ 39 at 54 (Pauline Books & Media 2006) (available as of Mar. 20, 2022 at https://tinyurl.com/5byyc7yd).

[79] *Divine Intimacy*, at 741.

[80] 1 Timothy 2:4, RSV-CE.

[81] 1 Thessalonians 4:3.

Second, we should firmly hope that God will help us. It is a dogmatic truth that "all ought to place and repose a most firm hope in God's help."[82] "[H]e who promised is faithful."[83] The Scriptures repeatedly teach us this truth:

> *Commit your way to the Lord; trust in him, and he will act. (Psalm 37:5, RSV-CE).*

> *Trust in him, and he will help you; make your ways straight, and hope in him. (Sirach 2:6, RSV-CE).*

> *I, the Lord your God, hold your right hand; it is I who say to you, "Fear not, I will help you." (Isaiah. 41:13, RSV-CE)*

> *The Lord is good and giveth strength in the day of trouble: and knoweth them that hope in him. (Nahum 1:7, Douay-Rheims).*

Third, we should firmly hope that God desires good for us. Start by standing on Scriptural promises that God has good plans for you. Here are several promises that you can meditate on in your prayer time:

> *For I know the plans I have for you, says the Lord, plans for welfare and not for evil, to give you a future and a hope. (Jeremiah 29:11, RSV-CE).*

---

82 Council of Trent, Session 6, "Canons Concerning Justification, 13 January, 1547," Ch. 13 "On the gift of Perseverance."

83 Hebrews 10:23, RSV-CE.

*There is hope for your future, says the Lord. (Jeremiah 31:17, RSV-CE).*

*The hope of the righteous ends in gladness. (Proverbs 10:28, RSV-CE).*

There was a recent time in my life where my hope in God was severely tested. Over fifteen years, my law firm had grown to nine attorneys, six staff and three offices around the country. The year 2018, however, started with the departure of a junior attorney and was followed with the sudden resignation of my most senior and long-serving attorney. As the year progressed, the shock waves continued. Our cases dried up. Clients sent work to other law firms. Just when I thought things were stabilizing, my second most senior and long-serving attorney resigned. At one point during the crisis, a friend asked my wife how I was doing. Her reply? *"Well, he hasn't talked about killing himself."* It was tough!

Things continued to change quickly. The loss in revenue made it impossible to support our overhead. I found a new tenant to sublet my Austin office space and negotiated a buyout of my office leases in Los Angeles and Northern Virginia. I had to lay off several staff. Others resigned. Slowly we brought long-term vendor contracts to a close that no longer fit our needs and found newer vendors to partner with who were willing to be flexible with a smaller organization.

As things progressed through 2018 and 2019, I began to describe the process as flying a large airplane through a terrible storm. The storm was forcing a rapid descent and the plane was being buffeted heavily. I was concerned that we would crash straight into the ground.

In the midst of this difficult trial, I had to make a choice. Would I continue to trust in God in the face of this adversity? Would I continue to obey God even if He did not appear to be answering my prayers?

Talking to a friend about the situation one night, I declared my choice — having made a decision to serve God I was not going to turn back now. "I am not going back." I was going to trust Him no matter how things turned out — **even if** things did not go the way I wanted them to.

I found strength for this commitment in the Bible. The life of Job, who resolved to trust God in the midst of his fiery trials, provided inspiration during the most difficult of times: *"Although he should kill me, I will trust in him."*[84]

I was also encouraged by the preaching of my spiritual mentor, who admonished us that we must serve God **even if** he does not seem to answer our prayers. This was the lesson of the three young men in the Book of Daniel who refused to bow down to the golden image and

---

[84] Job 13:15 (Douay-Rheims). In January 2024, I went on a retreat in Malvern, Pennsylvania. Every retreatant had a single room for the weekend and every room was dedicated to a saint. The name of the saint on the door of my room for the weekend was St. Job.

were thrown into the fiery furnace as a result. They replied to the king that **even if** God did not save them from the furnace, they would not serve his god or worship the golden statue!

> *Shadrach, Meshach, and Abednego answered King Nebuchadnezzar, "There is no need for us to defend ourselves before you in this matter. If our God, whom we serve, can save us from the white-hot furnace and from your hands, O king, may he save us! But* **even if** *he will not, you should know, O king, that we will not serve your god or worship the golden statue which you set up."*[85]

Into the fire they went! But God sent an angel to protect them, and they walked out of the fiery furnace unharmed, praising God.

In my life, things gradually calmed down and stabilized. By the beginning of March 2020, I realized that the plane had pulled its nose up at the last minute and made a soft landing. The firm was now two lawyers, two staff, and no offices. We were an entirely virtual law firm. Things were financially stable.

And then the country was locked down for COVID. No one was expecting that.

I was immediately thankful to God for having positioned the law firm for the pandemic. Looking back

---

[85] Daniel 3:16-18 (NABRE).

now, I can see clearly that God was positioning me and my law firm in anticipation of the pandemic. In fact, He re-shaped the firm in multiple ways that make us a better organization, that help us to more effectively serve our clients, and to be a good employer for the people who work for us. Only God could have known how to restructure my business for the surprises we faced in 2020 and to make us a better organization. I certainly was not mentally or spiritually prepared to downsize and radically change the firm voluntarily in the ways that turned out to be necessary to get where we needed to be.

How do you develop trust in God? It has to be developed through experience. We have to experience in our concrete circumstances of life that God is faithful. That He will provide. That He can be trusted. It is in the crucible that we grow in our trust in God. It is this foundation of trust that gives us hope in God for the future.

You can also reflect upon examples from salvation history of God's deliverance to ground your hope on. God allowed Joseph to be taken into captivity in Egypt, only to raise him up to save Israel from famine.[86] God saw the afflictions of the Israelites and sent Moses to lead them out

[86] Genesis chs. 37-47.

of Egypt.[87] God raised up Esther to become queen and save the Jews from the wicked plan of Haman.[88]

The story of Susanna in Chapter 13 of the Book of Daniel is another great story of how God saves those who hope in Him. Susanna was a beautiful woman who feared the Lord. Two lecherous old men, judges and elders of Israel who were consumed with lust for her, hid in her husband's garden one day as she prepared to bathe. When her servants had left and locked the garden, the two men approached her and said, "Look, the garden doors are shut, no one sees us, and we are in love with you; so give your consent, and lie with us. If you refuse, we will testify against you that a young man was with you, and this was why you sent your maids away."[89] Susanna refused, choosing to fall into their trap rather than sin before God. After Susanna cried out, the two men lodged their accusation against her. The next day, there was a trial before the assembly for adultery, which was punishable by death. The assembly believed the two elders and condemned her to death.

Susanna cried out in prayer to God, and the Holy Spirit touched a young man named Daniel. Daniel proclaimed to the assembly, "I am innocent of the blood

---

87 Exodus 3:7-10.

88 *See generally* Esther chs. 1-10.

89 Daniel 13:20-21, RSV-CE.

of this woman."[90] Recognizing in the spirit that an innocent woman had been condemned, Daniel proposed a cross-examination of the two accusers separate from each other.

Daniel cross-examined the first, asking under what tree they found her in adultery. A mastic tree, the first elder replied. They took him apart and brought the second elder. Asked the same question, he answered an evergreen oak. "Then all the assembly shouted loudly and blessed God, **who saves those who hope in him**."[91] The two elders were put to death for false witness instead of innocent Susanna.

God's plans for you are good — hope in God!

As you reflect on the scriptural promises and stories of hope, ask the Holy Spirit to personalize the message of hope for you. When you meditate on the passage, "There is hope for your future, says the Lord," imagine the Lord saying this directly to you. Put your name in if it helps: "Eric, there is hope for your future." Let the Holy Spirit minister hope to you through the living Word of God.

God has given us a gift of the Holy Spirit to aid us here — the gift of fear of the Lord.[92] The gift of fear of the

---

[90] Daniel 13:46, RSV-CE.

[91] Daniel 13:60, RSV-CE.

[92] *Effective Intercession for Our Loved Ones*, at 38-39 (discussing the fear of the Lord in the context of the "power tool" of respect).

Lord perfects the virtue of hope.[93] This gift is a filial fear, a fear that does not want to offend a loving Father. As we grow in this reverential fear of God and strive to avoid offending Him, it extinguishes in us a desire for earthly things and "urges us to a life of total self-detachment."[94] As we are stripped of our selfish proud desires, cupidity and concern for worldly things, this gift "gradually establishes in us perfect poverty of spirit."[95]

Poverty of spirit is the Beatitude that corresponds to the power tool of hope. The promise to the poor in spirit is possession of the kingdom of heaven, the object of our hope!

> *"Blessed are the poor in spirit, for theirs is the kingdom of heaven." (Matthew 5:3, RSV-CE).*

To be poor in spirit is to be humble of mind and heart.[96] Humility is a foundational virtue and Beatitude.[97] Thus, this Beatitude addresses "those who recognize their need for God and his grace."[98]

---

[93] *Divine Intimacy,* at 896.

[94] *Id.* at 898.

[95] *Id.*

[96] *Haydock Bible,* note on Matthew 5:3, at 1254.

[97] *Effective Intercession for Our Loved Ones,* at 51-57.

[98] *Ignatius Bible,* note on Matthew 5:3.

As we pray for hope and allow the Holy Spirit to strengthen our spirit in this area, we are adding the next piece of our spiritual armor for the battle. Hope is part of our spiritual armor. St. Paul tells us to "put on . . . for a helmet the hope of salvation."[99] Hope in God is also our buckler[100] or shield.

> *Every word of God is fire tried: he is a buckler to them that hope in him. (Proverbs 30:5, Douay-Rheims).*

> *Thou art my hiding place and my shield; I hope in thy word. (Psalm 119:114, RSV-CE).*

Hope in God is an essential part of our spiritual protection. If we do not have a helmet and shield in the spirit, the enemy can attack our thoughts freely. Our thought life is where the enemy attacks. The fiery darts of the enemy can strike us at will without a shield. When you are struck with temptation or discouragement, make an act of hope in God, and armor up again!

Ultimately, we place our hope in our Saviour, Jesus Christ. In the fullness of time, God sent His Son Jesus Christ

---

[99] 1 Thessalonians 5:8, RSV-CE; *see also* Ephesians 6:17 ("take the helmet of salvation").

[100] A buckler is a small round shield held by a handle or worn on the forearm.

> *to redeem those who were under the law, so that we might receive adoption as sons. And because you are sons, God has sent the Spirit of his Son into our hearts, crying, "Abba! Father!" So through God you are no longer a slave but a son, and if a son then an heir. (Galatians 4:4-7, RSV-CE).*

Do not give into temptation, discouragement or however the enemy may be attacking you. Be heroic in your hope! "Make it a habit to say many times a day, 'Father, I trust you.'"[101] You will be blessed if you stand firm in your hope in God.

> *Blessed is he whose heart does not condemn him, and who has not given up his hope. (Sirach 14:2, RSV-CE).*

My prayer for you today is that "the God of hope fill you with all joy and peace in believing, so that by the power of the Holy Spirit you may abound in hope."[102] May you abound in hope in Jesus' Name! Amen.

---

[101] Peter Kreeft, *Practical Theology: Spiritual Direction from St. Thomas Aquinas*, at 41 (Ignatius Press) (2014).

[102] Romans 15:13, RSV-CE.

## Additional Resources

Related Scriptures:

1 Sam. 30; Ps. 42:5, 43:5, 125:1; Proverbs 3:5; Sir. 2, 34:13; Lam. 3:24; Isaiah 30:15; Jer. 17:7; Romans 8:24-25, 12:12; 1 Tim. 1:1; Heb. 3:6; 1 Peter 1:13, 21.

Douay-Rheims translation: Ps. 90:9; Ecclesiasticus (Sirach) 24:24, 34:16; Job 13:15.

Songs:

*"My Prayer For You"* — Song by Alisa Turner from the album *Alisa Turner* (Released 2017).
(A YouTube video of the song can be watched here: https://tinyurl.com/y5uaboze.)

*"Speak Life"* — Song by TobyMac from the album *Eye on It* (Released 2012).
(A YouTube video of the song can be watched here: https://tinyurl.com/y6a4v7ht.)

Prayer:

Rosary, Second Glorious Mystery — The Ascension (*Mark 16:19-20*) (Fruit of the mystery: hope).

Act of Hope:

> *O my God, relying on Thy almighty power and infinite mercy and promises, I hope to obtain pardon of my sins, the help of Thy grace, and Life Everlasting, through the merits of Jesus Christ, my Lord and Redeemer.*

Additional Reading:

CCC § 1817-21, 1843, 2091-92, 2657-58.

Additional Points for Reflection:

Journey to the Promised Land:  Exodus 3:7-10.

Armor of God:  Ephesians 6:17.

Beatitude:  Matthew 5:3.

Gift of the Holy Spirit:  Fear of the Lord.

# The Power of Praise

## Promise in God's Word

*I call upon the Lord who is worthy to be praised and I am saved from my enemies. (Psalm 18:3, RSV-CE).*

## Reflection

What is praise?

*Praise is the form of prayer which recognizes most immediately that God is God. It lauds God for his own sake and gives him glory, quite beyond what he does, but simply because HE IS.*[103]

God is worthy to be praised because of who HE IS. This is something we constantly forget. Praise comes easy when God blesses us! But when darkness surrounds us, praise does not escape our lips. We need to re-orient our perspective on praise and make it about God instead of about our situation.

Where do we find the words we need to praise God? Start with the Word of God itself! The Bible teaches us how to praise God. There are many psalms of praise that we can offer as a prayer of praise to God, using words

---

[103] CCC § 2639; *see also* CCC §§ 2640-2643, 2649.

inspired by the Holy Spirit.[104] Many praise and worship songs today use the words of the psalms.

The three men in the fiery furnace gave praise to God in the midst of the flames.[105] David gave praise to God after the people of Israel made their offerings for the building of the temple.[106] Tobit composed a prayer of praise and thanks to God after having his sight restored with the assistance of the Archangel Raphael.[107] Judith offered a hymn of praise after the defeat of the Assyrians.[108]

> *We praise God by recalling His marvelous deeds. (Cassiodorus)*

My mother passed away in 2016 after a nine-week battle with lung cancer. As long as my father's battle with cancer had been, my mother's was brief. She did not want to go through what he had endured. She had remarried and moved to the wine country in Northern California in the intervening years. Our relationship had been up and down as a result (family is complicated). With the cancer diagnosis, we were able to re-establish a closer relationship over several brief visits out to California.

---

104 *See* Additional Resources at the end of this chapter for a list.

105 Daniel 3:28-68 (RSV-CE); Daniel 3:51-90 (Douay-Rheims).

106 1 Chronicles 29:10-13.

107 Tobit 13:1-11.

108 Judith 16:1-16.

As she began hospice care, updates came from her husband periodically. I had a trip scheduled to Southern California for a deposition. That morning, feeling spiritually low, I went to a nearby church and went to confession. I left feeling better and ready to focus on preparing for the deposition. Late afternoon, the phone rang. It was my mother's husband calling to tell me that she was not doing well. The hospice nurse thought that she would be passing away today.

I called home. A decision had to be made quickly. Should I try and get to Northern California tonight? We found a flight leaving Orange County in an hour. My hotel was across the street from the airport. I packed and rushed over. I returned the rental car, took the shuttle bus, went through security, hurried to the gate, and walked on the plane. A few minutes later, the door closed and we pushed back and departed to San Jose. On the flight, I found a rental car and mapped out the drive. I would be arriving in San Jose around 9pm. It was a two-and-a-half hour drive from there to her home in Healdsburg. I would be lucky to get there by midnight if there was no traffic in the Bay Area. It was already late at night when I picked up the rental car (a familiar experience to a road warrior) and began the drive around the Bay.

Close to midnight, I pulled up to the house. I had been praying continually since I received the call from her husband, and now I wondered — did I make it? What would I find when I came into the house? I prayed, "God's will be done."

I entered the house and climbed the stairs. It was immediately apparent to me that my mother was still alive, but was in a panic. Her eyes were closed, the hospital bed they had brought in was propped up, she was breathing rapidly, and she appeared to be in a state of panic. I knew that the one thing she feared most from an episode my father had in the hospital was suffocating to death. I approached the bed, and said, "Mom, it's Eric. I'm here." She immediately sat straight up in the bed and cried out.

I brought a chair next to the bed and began to pray out loud. As the prayers started, her body started to relax. Her breathing became calm. I prayed the Divine Mercy chaplet. I pulled out my breviary and began to pray Compline (Night Prayer). Near the end of Compline is the *Nunc dimíttis*:

> *"Nunc dimíttis ✠ servum tuum, Dómine, * secúndum verbum tuum in pace: Quia vidérunt óculi mei * salutáre tuum, Quod parásti * ante fáciem ómnium populórum, Lumen ad revelatiónem géntium, * et glóriam plebis tuæ Israël."*
>
> *"**Lord, now lettest thou thy servant depart in peace, according to thy word;*** for *mine eyes have seen thy salvation which thou hast prepared in the presence of all peoples, a light for revelation to the Gentiles, and for glory to thy people Israel."*
>
> She passed away in peace.

In God's providence, He put together what seemed to be an extremely improbable chain of events to allow me to be physically and spiritually present for my mother's passing. I happened to already be in California, I had spiritually prepared myself that morning with the sacrament of confession, I caught the last flight north on an hour's notice, I drove around the Bay Area without hitting construction or traffic, and I arrived in the middle of the night while my mother was still alive. After this long and improbable journey, we spent a brief hour together there in prayer. Peace had entered the room. My mother was then able to pass away peacefully to be with God.

I tell you this story to give praise to God. What marvelous deeds has God done in your life? Surely each of us has been blessed by God at some point in our life. Bring His marvelous deeds to mind and give Him praise.

> *We praise God by recalling His marvelous deeds. (Cassiodorus)*

Praise is the breakout tool as we pray for ourselves. Truth, integrity, patience and hope have laid the foundation. Now, praise is the first step offensively as we go into battle. You may be thinking, what does praising God for who HE IS have to do with me? The power of praise is counter-intuitive, but it is real.

There are many biblical examples of praise being used as a weapon in spiritual warfare. We will look at one from the Old Testament, and one from the New

Testament, to show that the power tool of praise is something constant across salvation history.

We see one example in the Old Testament at a time when a great multitude of Moabites and Ammonites were coming against Israel. King Jehoshaphat proclaimed a fast, prayed to God and consulted the prophets. "When he had taken counsel with the people, he appointed those who were to sing to the Lord and praise him in holy array, as they went before the army."[109] Then we see the power of praise in battle:

> *When they began to sing and praise, the Lord set an ambush against the men of Ammon, Moab, and Mount Se'ir, who had come against Judah, so that they were routed. . . . When Judah came to the watchtower of the wilderness, they looked toward the multitude; and behold, they were dead bodies lying on the ground; none had escaped. (2 Chronicles 20:22, 24, RSV-CE).*

Rightfully so, the Israelites continued to praise God after the victory. But it is in the praise *before* the victory, staring in the face of a vast enemy, that we find the proper orientation for praise in spiritual warfare.

We also see the power of praise in the New Testament. Paul and Silas were evangelizing in Philippi of Macedonia when Paul's prayers delivered a slave girl

---

[109] 2 Chronicles 20:21, RSV-CE.

of a spirit of divination.[110] Her owners, now despoiled of their means of income, dragged Paul and Silas before the local magistrates and charged them with disturbing the peace of the city. At the order of the magistrates, Paul and Silas were flogged with rods and thrown in prison.[111]

After being beaten and thrown in prison, did Paul and Silas complain? No — they praised God! And once again, we see God move in power to save them from their enemies:

> *About midnight Paul and Silas were praying and singing hymns to God, and the prisoners were listening to them, and suddenly there was a great earthquake, so that the foundations of the prison were shaken; and immediately all the doors were opened and every one's fetters were unfastened. (Acts 16:25-26, RSV-CE).*

Not only were Paul and Silas freed, but the jailer and his family received salvation and baptism as a result of the miracle! Praise God!

We also see today that there is a connection between praise and deliverance from our enemies. Fr. Gabriele Amorth, formerly the chief exorcist for the Diocese of Rome, noted that "Prayers of praise — both spontaneous and especially biblical, such as the Psalms and hymns of

---

110 Acts 16:12, 16-18.

111 Acts 16:19-24.

praise to God — are most beneficial" in bringing about liberation from evil spirits.[112] The Scriptures support this conclusion as well.

After the prophet Samuel anointed David as king of Israel in place of Saul (who had failed to obey God), the Scripture says that "The Spirit of the Lord departed from Saul, and an evil spirit from the Lord tormented him."[113] Saul's servants recognized that an evil spirit was tormenting the king, and recommended he seek a musician to perform before him to help drive away the spirit. At the suggestion of one of the servants, Saul sent for David. At the call of the king, David entered his service and the favor of God was upon him. Here we see the teaching about the power of praise:

> *And whenever the evil spirit from God was upon Saul, David took the lyre and played it with his hand; so Saul was refreshed, and was well, and the evil spirit departed from him. (1 Samuel 16:23, RSV-CE).*

St. Paul's teaching on the armor of God confirms the place of praise in our prayer life:

> *[B]e filled with the Spirit, addressing one another in psalms and hymns and spiritual songs, singing and*

---

[112] Fr. Gabriele Amorth, *An Exorcist Tells His Story*, at 50 (Ignatius Press 1999).

[113] 1 Samuel 16:14, RSV-CE.

*making melody to the Lord with all your heart. (Ephesians 5:18-19, RSV-CE).*

The psalmist links the high praises of God with a powerful weapon, the two-edged sword:

*Let the high praises of God be in their throats and two-edged swords in their hands, to wreak vengeance on the nations and chastisement on the peoples, to bind their kings with chains and their nobles with fetters of iron, to execute on them the judgment written! (Psalm 149:6-9, RSV-CE).*

In spiritual warfare, what is that two-edged sword? It is the Word of God!

*For the word of God is living and active, sharper than any two-edged sword, piercing to the division of soul and spirit, of joints and marrow, and discerning the thoughts and intentions of the heart. (Heb. 4:12, RSV-CE).*

The Word of God is the sword of the Spirit:

*And take the helmet of salvation, and the sword of the Spirit, which is the word of God. (Ephesians 6:17, RSV-CE).*

Take up the Word of God and begin fighting!

Ultimately, we have to choose to praise God and not curse Him. We need to think about what we say. Our Lord Jesus Christ tells us that "On the day of judgment men will render account for every careless word they utter."[114] Are we using our voice to praise God? There is power in the words that we speak:

> *Death and life are in the power of the tongue. (Proverbs 18:21, RSV-CE).*

Use your voice to praise God and speak life!

My prayer for you is that God would grant you a divine re-orientation of your perspective on praise, that He would enlighten your mind as to who HE IS, that He would open your spirit to praise Him, and that you would be delivered from all your enemies, in the Name of Jesus! Amen.

---

[114] Matthew 12:36, RSV-CE.

## Additional Resources

Related Scriptures:

2 Chron. 20; Job 38:4-7; Ps. 20:7-8, 22:3, 149:6-9; Jonah 2; Ephesians 5:19; Col. 3:16.

Praise Psalms: 18, 95, 100, 105, 107, 145, 147-150.

The "sacrifice of praise" – Heb. 13:15; Psalm 49:14 (Douay-Rheims).

Songs:

*"King of Kings"* — Song by Hillsong Worship from the album *Awake* (Released 2019).
(A YouTube video of the song can be watched here: https://tinyurl.com/yyhm7tcy.)

*"Goodness of God"* — Song by Bethel Music & Jenn Johnson from the album *Victory* (Released 2019).
(A YouTube video of the song can be watched here: https://tinyurl.com/ssd69uc.)

*"Praise You In This Storm"* — Song by Natalie Grant from the album *No Stranger* (Released 2020).
(A YouTube video of the song can be watched here: https://tinyurl.com/y323kj8h.)

*"How Great Thou Art"* — Song by the Brooklyn Tabernacle Choir from the album *Hymns & Voices* (Released 1995).
(A YouTube video of the song can be watched here: https://tinyurl.com/y465uxs7.)

*"Hallelujah You're Worthy"* — Song by The Brooklyn Tabernacle Choir from the album *I'll Say Yes* (Released 2017).
(A YouTube recording of the song can be heard here: https://tinyurl.com/rpvuuset.)

Prayer:

*The Divine Praises (Laudes Divina)*

*Blessed be God. Blessed be His Holy Name. Blessed be Jesus Christ, true God and true Man. Blessed be the Name of Jesus. Blessed be His Most Sacred Heart. Blessed be His Most Precious Blood. Blessed be Jesus in the Most Holy Sacrament of the Altar. Blessed be the Holy Ghost, the Paraclete. Blessed be the great Mother of God, Mary most Holy. Blessed be her Holy and Immaculate Conception. Blessed be her Glorious Assumption. Blessed be the name of Mary, Virgin and Mother. Blessed be St. Joseph, her most chaste spouse. Blessed be God in His Angels and in His Saints. Amen.*

*May the heart of Jesus, in the Most Blessed Sacrament, be praised, adored, and loved with grateful affection, at every moment, in all the tabernacles of the world, even to the end of time. Amen.*

Additional Points for Reflection:

Journey to the Promised Land: Exodus ch. 15.

Armor of God: Ephesians 5:18-20.

Beatitude: Matthew 5:12.

Gift of the Holy Spirit: Understanding.

# The Power of Love

## Promise in God's Word

*There is no fear in love, but perfect love casts out fear. (1 John 4:18, RSV-CE).*

## Reflection

Fear is one of the greatest weapons of the enemy today. Fear is debilitating. Fear affects our ability to think clearly. Fear is a major obstacle to us obtaining "saving faith."[115] Fear kills our hope.

Christians are not supposed to be people of fear! The phrase "fear not" (or similar words) is the most-repeated advice in the Holy Bible.[116] So how do we fight fear? With perfect love.

Before we can love others, however, we have to be firmly rooted in the belief that God loves us. Oftentimes that means we have to start by realizing and accepting that we are lovable. This can be difficult for those of us who have suffered at the hands of those who should be loving us. It can be difficult to accept that God loves us in light

---

115 Rev. Bro. Augustine Momoh, O.P., *Step Into The Flames and Rescue Souls*, at 20 (Newborne Enterprises 1997).

116 *E.g.*, Genesis 26:24; Ex. 20:20; Deut. 31:6; Joshua 1:9; Isaiah 35:4, 43:1, 54:4; Matthew 1:20, 6:34, 17:6-7; Luke 1:12-13, 12:7; John 6:20, 14:27; Revelation 2:10.

of our sins. And yet, it is foundational truth that God loves each of us individually.

*As the Father has loved me, so have I loved you. (John 15:9, RSV-CE).*

If you are doubting or hesitating, stop for a minute and reflect on this. Have you ever loved someone? Is there anyone who has not loved another person? Do you love your mother? Father? Brother? Sister? Husband? Wife? Children? Is there a relative you love? Someone who was kind to you? Think about the people you love or have loved.

Are you with me so far?

With that in mind, we read in the Bible:

*"We love, because He first loved us." (1 John 4:19, RSV-CE).*

Repeat that to yourself again.

Now, realize that if you love someone, or have loved someone, then you know that God has loved you first. You do not need to ever wonder, "Does God love me?" You have this Scriptural assurance that He does.

Ultimately, it is not intellectual knowledge that God loves us that casts out fear. Rather, it is encountering the love of God and being transformed by it. It is through our daily discipline of prayer that we learn to open ourselves to the love of God through the Holy Spirit. Indeed, this is the point of Christian prayer — disposing ourselves to receive God's love.[117]

Take this to prayer, because it is so foundational to your ability to pray for yourself. There are many other Scriptures that you can read and reflect upon in order to let God's love permeate you.[118] Go ahead and make time in your life this week to do so.

You can read each passage separately, prayerfully reflecting on what it says, putting it in the first person and letting it apply to you. Then, listen in your heart for God to speak. Love requires listening.

> *I will allure her, and bring her into the wilderness, and speak tenderly to her. (Hosea 2:14, RSV-CE).*

The love of God is part of our spiritual armor. One view is that the love of God is the helmet of salvation.[119] "Our thoughts must be deeply rooted in faith and hope in His great love for us!"[120] Upon reflection, I think that another part of the armor also fits well here:

---

[117] *See* Torkington, *The Primacy of Loving* (Circle Books 2023).

[118] *See* Wisdom 11:24; Isaiah 49:15-16; John 3:16, 15:9, 16:27; Romans 5:8; 1 John 3:1, 4:7-8.

[119] Ephesians 6:17.

[120] Mother Nadine Brown, *God's Armor*, at 89 (Intercessors of the Lamb 1998).

*[S]hod your feet with the equipment of the Gospel of peace. (Ephesians 6:15, RSV-CE).*

The gospel is the good news of God's love for us. "[T]hrough the gospel peace is proclaimed to us."[121] The good news is that God sent His only begotten Son to make atonement for our sins, to open heaven to us, the descendants of Adam and Eve, who were cast out of their place of intimacy with God because of their sin. We become children of God the Father by the waters of baptism and are re-admitted to intimacy with Him. "[Y]ou who were once far off have been brought near in the blood of Christ."[122]

It is only when our hearts are firmly rooted in the peace of God that we can fully surrender to His overwhelming love for us. We must draw near to God in prayer, for He will draw near to us.[123] He will speak to us in the silence of our hearts.[124] God will speak words of love to you:

*I created you in my own image and likeness.*[125]

---

[121] *Id.* (referencing Matthew 10:12).

[122] Ephesians 2:13, RSV-CE.

[123] James 4:8.

[124] Mother Teresa, *In the Heart of the World: Thoughts, Stories and Prayers* (2002).

[125] Genesis 1:27.

*Before you were in the womb, I knew you.*[126]

*You are my child.*[127]

*I rejoice over you with singing.*[128]

*Every hair on your head is numbered.*[129]

*You are the apple of my eye.*[130]

*You are engraved on the palm of my hand.*[131]

*I died for you.*[132]

*If you seek me with all your heart, you will find me.*[133]

*One day I will wipe away every tear from your eyes.*[134]

My prayer for you is that as you pray and meditate on God's love for you, that God will heal and remove from your spirit every obstacle to receiving His love for you. As

---

126 Jeremiah 1:5.

127 1 John 3:1.

128 Zephaniah 3:17.

129 Luke 12:7.

130 Deut. 32:10.

131 Isaiah 49:16.

132 Romans 5:8.

133 Deut. 4:29.

134 Revelation 21:3-4.

these obstacles are removed, I pray that God's love be poured into your heart by the Holy Spirit and you receive healing and deliverance from all fear in the Name of Jesus. Amen.

## What is Peace?

- Peace is, before God formed you in the womb, He knew you.[135]
- Peace is, you are God's child.[136]
- Peace is, even the hairs on your head are numbered.[137]
- Peace is, you are more valuable than many sparrows.[138]
- Peace is, your Heavenly Father knows everything that you need.[139]
- Peace is, the Holy Spirit helps you in your weakness.[140]

---

135 Jeremiah 1:5.

136 1 John 3:1.

137 Matthew 10:30.

138 Matthew 10:31.

139 Matthew 6:32.

140 Romans 8:26.

- Peace is, while you were yet a sinner Christ died for you.[141]
- Peace is, the kingdom of God is within you.[142]
- Peace is, you are a temple of the Holy Spirit.[143]
- Peace is, the Father and the Son have come to dwell within you.[144]
- Peace is, there are many mansions in heaven and Jesus has gone to prepare a place for you.[145]
- Peace is, we know that in everything God works for good with those who love him.[146]
- Peace is, in the world you have tribulation; but be of good cheer, Jesus has overcome the world.[147]
- Peace is, nothing can separate you from the love of God in Christ Jesus our Lord.[148]

---

141 Romans 5:8.

142 Luke 17:20-21.

143 1 Corinthians 6:19-20.

144 John 14:10, 20.

145 John 14:2.

146 Romans 8:28.

147 John 16:33.

148 Romans 8:35-39.

Peace is a gift to you from Jesus himself. Listen to Jesus speak to you now:

*"Do not let your hearts be troubled. You believe in God; believe also in me. My Father's house has many rooms; if that were not so, would I have told you that I am going there to prepare a place for you? And if I go and prepare a place for you, I will come back and take you to be with me that you also may be where I am. You know the way to the place where I am going."*

*"I am the way and the truth and the life. No one comes to the Father except through me."*

*"I will not leave you as orphans; I will come to you. . . . Because I live, you also will live. On that day you will realize that I am in my Father, and you are in me, and I am in you."*

*"Peace I leave with you; my peace I give to you; not as the world gives do I give to you. Let not your hearts be troubled, neither let them be afraid."*[149]

*"I have said this to you, that in me you may have peace."*[150]

"May the peace of Christ rule in your hearts, to which you were called in one body."[151] Peace be with you.

---

[149] John ch. 14.

[150] John 16:33.

[151] Colossians 3:15.

## Additional Resources

Related Scriptures:

Sir. 34:16-17; Joshua 1:9; Matthew 5:43-48; John 15:12-17, 13:34-35, 14:21-24; 1 Cor. 13; 1 John; 2 John 1:5-6; 2 Peter 1:5-7; Rev. 2:4-5.

Songs:

*"Jesus, I Need You"* — Song by Hillsong Worship from the album *OPEN HEAVEN / River Wild* (Released 2015). (A YouTube video of the song can be watched here: https://tinyurl.com/kr9ms3pj.)

Prayer:

Rosary, Second Joyful Mystery — The Visitation (*Luke 1:39-56*) (Fruit of the mystery: love of neighbor).

Act of Charity:

> *O my God, I love Thee above all things, with my whole heart and soul, because Thou art all-good and worthy of all love. I love my neighbor as myself for the love of Thee. I forgive all who have injured me, and ask pardon of all whom I have injured.*

Quote:

"Perfect love undertakes even the most difficult things."[152]

---

[152] St. Thomas Aquinas, Sermon 18 on the Saints (2d Nocturn at Matins, Sept. 8, Feast of Nativity of the Blessed Virgin Mary).

<u>Additional Points for Reflection:</u>

Journey to the Promised Land:  Exodus 34:6.

Armor of God:  Ephesians 6:15.

Beatitude:  Matthew 5:9.

Gift of the Holy Spirit:  Piety.

# The Power of Authority

## Promise in God's Word

*Behold, I have given you authority to tread upon serpents and scorpions, and over all the power of the enemy; and nothing shall hurt you. (Luke 10:19, RSV-CE).*

## Reflection

As baptized Christians, we have this authority from Jesus. Firmly rooted in God's love for us, with the full armor of God on, we are positioned to now step out in faith with the authority given to us by God. We want to use this authority in our spiritual combat against the devil and his agents. It comes with a promise of divine protection as well. He lives within us,[153] so have confidence in your spiritual authority!

What does it mean to have spiritual authority? Authority is generally "the moral or legal right or ability to control."[154] This is why divine authority is important when engaged in spiritual warfare against the fallen angels. Jesus had divine authority over the evil spirits, and they had to obey Him.

---

[153] John 14:23.

[154] Definition of "authority" in the *Cambridge Dictionary* (https://dictionary.cambridge.org/us/dictionary/english/authority).

> *"What is this? A new teaching! With authority he commands even the unclean spirits, and they obey him!" (Mark 1:27, RSV-CE).*

In contrast, we see what happened to the sons of Sceva, who only invoked the Name of Jesus as a talisman without being Christians. They lacked true divine authority, and it did not turn out well for them.

> *Then some of the itinerant Jewish exorcists undertook to pronounce the name of the Lord Jesus over those who had evil spirits, saying, "I adjure you by the Jesus whom Paul preaches." Seven sons of a Jewish high priest named Sceva were doing this. But the evil spirit answered them, "Jesus I know, and Paul I know; but who are you?" And the man in whom the evil spirit was leaped on them, mastered all of them, and overpowered them, so that they fled out of that house naked and wounded. (Acts 19:13-16, RSV-CE).*

The Bible makes a distinction between authority and power. It is helpful to understand the difference and apply it correctly to our prayer for ourselves.

> *And they were all amazed and said to one another, "What is this word? For with authority and power he commands the unclean spirits, and they come out." (Luke 4:36, RSV-CE).*

Here we see both words being used — authority <u>and</u> power. The Greek word translated here as authority is *exousia*. Exousia is also the word used in Mark 1:27, above.

The Greek word translated here as power, however, is *dynamis.*

Jesus told us that He possessed all authority in heaven and on earth:

> *"All authority [exousia] in heaven and on earth has been given to me." (Matthew 28:18, RSV-CE).*

Jesus delegated authority over evil spirits and for healing to His disciples:

> *And he called to him his twelve disciples and gave them authority [exousia] over unclean spirits, to cast them out, and to heal every disease and every infirmity. (Matthew 10:1, RSV-CE).*[155]

The Bible also tells us that Jesus was anointed by God with power:

> *God anointed Jesus of Nazareth with the Holy Spirit and with power [dynamis]; how he went about doing good and healing all that were oppressed by the devil, for God was with him. (Acts 10:38, RSV-CE).*

Jesus also gave this power to His disciples:

> *And he called the twelve together and gave them power [dynamis] and authority [exousia] over all demons and to cure diseases. (Luke 9:1, RSV-CE).*[156]

---

[155] *See also* Mark 6:7.

[156] *See also* Luke 10:19.

In turn, He has given all believers this same power. The Word of God confirms that God "gives power and strength to his people." (Ps. 68:35, RSV-CE). The power we are talking about here is the Anointing Power of the Holy Spirit. Dynamis is where we get the word "dynamite" from! Do you want spiritual dynamite in your prayers?

We see examples of this power manifested in the early Church:

> *And Stephen, full of grace and power [dynamis], did great wonders and signs among the people. (Acts 6:8, RSV-CE).*

With respect to power, the amount of anointing given to each person is different. "It is impossible for you to receive the anointing of God at a high level which your prayer life cannot sustain."[157] The following chapters in this book touch on different power tools that impact the spiritual power of one's prayers. For now, however, have confidence that Jesus has given you spiritual authority in your life. You are not helpless! Pray for yourself!

This power is still available to those who believe. So how do we apply what we just learned about authority and power to prayer for ourselves? How do we access this power tool?

---

[157] Rev. Bro. Augustine Momoh, O.P., *The Anointing Power*, at 61 (Newborne Enterprises) (2d ed. 1999).

In the divine and natural order, God has given each of us authority to pray for deliverance from evil spirits from our own bodies.[158] As baptized Christians, Jesus gave us authority over evil spirits. We need to grasp the concept of having this authority and use it.

> *"And these signs will accompany those who believe: in my name they will cast out demons; they will speak in new tongues; they will pick up serpents, and if they drink any deadly thing, it will not hurt them; they will lay their hands on the sick, and they will recover." (Mark 16:17-18, RSV-CE).*

There is a story in the New Testament about authority that is worth reflecting on. As Jesus was entering Capernaum, a centurion came to him about his servant, who was lying paralyzed at home. Jesus offered to come and heal him. The centurion responded, however:

> *Lord, I am not worthy to have you come under my roof; but only say the word, and my servant will be healed. For I am a man under authority [exousia], with soldiers under me; and I say to one, 'Go,' and he goes, and to another, 'Come,' and he comes, and to my slave, 'Do this,' and he does it." (Matthew 8:8-9, RSV-CE).*

---

[158] *Deliverance Prayers for the Laity*, at 7-8 (Sensus Traditionis Press 2017). Because this Power Tools book is focused on prayer for *ourselves only*, it does not go into the issues of who may have authority to pray for others for deliverance.

St. Matthew tells us that "when Jesus heard him, he marveled." "Not even in Israel have I found such faith." Jesus then told the centurion, "Go; be it done for you as you have believed." Of course, the servant was healed at that very moment!

The centurion's response to Jesus is a powerful statement of faith in the authority of Jesus. The centurion understood the essence of authority and he believed that Jesus had divine authority. "Only say the word and my servant will be healed."

Do we exercise our God-given authority appropriately in our life? Do we take authority over ourselves in the Name of Jesus, binding up all of the operations of the enemy in our lives in His Name? We are not helpless in the battle against Satan and his demons, but yet people perish for lack of knowledge.[159] We need to learn to pray aggressively for ourselves, and not sit passively waiting for God to do all the work.[160] May God grant you courage to exercise the authority that He has granted you in Christ Jesus!

---

[159] Hosea 4:6.

[160] For an example of a prayer for self-deliverance that exercises our God-given authority, see *Release Me O Lord Jesus* (cited in Additional Resources below).

## Prayer to Take Authority Over Yourself

*In the Name of Jesus, I take authority and I bind all powers and forces in the air, in the ground, in the water, in the underground, in the netherworld, in nature and in fire.*

*You are the Lord over the entire universe and I give you the Glory for your creation. In your Name I bind all demonic forces that have come against me and my family and I seal all of us in the protection of your Precious Blood that was shed for us on the Cross.*

*Mary, our mother, I seek your protection and intercession with the Sacred Heart of Jesus for me and my family. Surround us with your mantle of love to discourage the enemy.*

*St. Michael and our guardian angels come defend me and my family in battle against all the evil ones that roam the earth.*

*In the Name of Jesus I bind and command all the powers and forces of evil to depart right now away from me, my family, our homes and our lands. And I thank you Lord Jesus for you are a faithful and compassionate God.*

*Amen.*

## Additional Resources

Related Scriptures:

Num. 27:20; 2 Chron. 8:10; Sir. 17:2; Matthew 9:6, 8, 12:29, 21:23; Mark 2:10, 3:15, 23-27, 6:7, 16:17-18; Luke 9:1-2, 10:17-20, 11:14-23.

Songs:

*"Send Us Out"* — Song by John Michael Talbot from the album *Come Worship the Lord* (Sparrow Records 1990) (A YouTube video of the song can be watched here: https://tinyurl.com/mrxek3uw.)

*"More Love, More Power (Live)"* — Song by Michael W. Smith from the album *Worship* (Released 2001) (A YouTube video of the song can be watched here: https://tinyurl.com/3cdx8vpm.)

Additional Reading:

Fr. Chad Ripperger, *Deliverance Prayers for Use by the Laity* (Sensus Traditionis Press 2017) (available for order here: https://tinyurl.com/yy84b8uz.)

Rev. Bro. Augustine Momoh, O.P., *Release Me, O Lord Jesus* (Holy Spirit Power Revival Ministry 2002) (https://tinyurl.com/mbfpupa8) (Kindle).

Prayers online at *The Saint Michael Center for Spiritual Renewal* (https://tinyurl.com/3m5pry49.)

Additional Points for Reflection:

Journey to the Promised Land: Exodus 34:10.

Armor of God: Ephesians 6:10.

Beatitude: *See* Luke 10:17-20.

Gift of the Holy Spirit: Knowledge.

# The Power of the Blood of Jesus

## Promise in God's Word

*As for you also, because of the blood of my covenant with you, I will set your captives free from the waterless pit. Return to your stronghold, O prisoners of hope; today I declare that I will restore to you double. (Zechariah 9:11-12, RSV-CE).*

## Reflection

Captives are set free by the Blood of Jesus! The prophet foretold the power in the blood of the new covenant, the blood shed by Jesus on the cross. If there is some portion of your life that is still in captivity, you need to plead the Blood of Jesus over it for freedom and deliverance.

The true power in the Blood of Jesus comes from receiving Jesus in Holy Communion.[161] During His public ministry, Jesus boldly proclaimed to the people the shocking truth that one must eat His flesh and drink His blood to have supernatural life:

*"Truly, truly, I say to you, unless you eat the flesh of the Son of man and drink his blood, you have no*

---

[161] Jesus is fully present in Holy Communion under both species of bread and wine. CCC 1390. Thus, one who receives Holy Communion under the form of bread also receives the Precious Blood.

> *life in you; he who eats my flesh and drinks my blood has eternal life, and I will raise him up at the last day. For my flesh is food indeed, and my blood is drink indeed. He who eats my flesh and drinks my blood abides in me, and I in him." (John 6:53-56, RSV-CE).*

Those listening to Jesus understood that He was speaking literally, not figuratively. But they could not grasp the spiritual meaning of His words. The Jews recoiled when Jesus first said this — "How can this man give us his flesh to eat?"[162] Rather than explain away what He said, however, Jesus doubled down with the quote above. In fact, after being challenged, Jesus switched to a different word for "eat" here in the ancient Greek. That word, *trōgō,* means to chew or gnaw. This truly shocked those who were present to hear.

The Bread of Life discourse also led to the falling away of many of His disciples.[163] Did Jesus call them back and try to explain that He was only speaking symbolically? No. His words stand: "Unless you eat the flesh of the Son of man and drink his blood, you have no life in you."

The Church's belief in the Real Presence of Christ in the Eucharist (Holy Communion) goes back to the Last

---

[162] John 6:52, RSV-CE.

[163] John 6:66. This is the only example in the gospels of large numbers of followers leaving Jesus.

Supper.[164] At the Last Supper, Jesus changed the bread and wine into His Body and Blood, proclaiming, "This is My Body. This is My Blood."[165] The universal and traditional belief in the Real Presence was attested to by the Fathers of the Church.[166] The sharpest controversy over the Real Presence did not even arise until the Reformation in the 16th Century. Even Martin Luther acknowledged in 1532, however, that the whole of Christendom believed in the Real Presence.[167]

For those of us who continue to believe in the Real Presence and receive Holy Communion, we must receive the Body and Blood of Christ with attention, devotion and a conscience clean of serious sin. St. Paul gives us a stern warning about receiving unworthily:

> *Whoever, therefore, eats the bread or drinks the cup of the Lord in an unworthy manner will be guilty of profaning the body and blood of the Lord. Let a man*

---

[164] The Roman Catholic Church has held this belief since the Last Supper, as it holds that Christ ordained the apostles as priests at that time and said the first Mass. Despite their split from Rome in the Great Schism of 1054, the Eastern Orthodox likewise retain the belief in the Real Presence of Christ in the Eucharist.

[165] Matthew 26:26-29; Mark 14:22-25; Lk. 22:14-20; *see also* 1 Corinthians 10:16, 11:23-26.

[166] Phle, Joseph, *The Real Presence of Christ in the Eucharist,* The Catholic Encyclopedia, Vol. 5 (Robert Appleton Co., NY 1909). Last retrieved Dec. 22, 2023, at http://www.newadvent.org/cathen/05573a.htm.

[167] *Id.*

> *examine himself, and so eat of the bread and drink of the cup. For any one who eats and drinks without discerning the body eats and drinks judgment upon himself. That is why many of you are weak and ill, and some have died.* (*1 Corinthians 11:27-30, RSV-CE*).

For many years, I did not listen to St. Paul's warning. I received Holy Communion with little attention to what I was doing. I would receive even when I had not attended Mass in months and had not been to confession. May the Lord have mercy on me!

After my return to the Church, I began to pay more attention to these things. Even though I was not receiving to my judgment, there were times when I received Holy Communion without reverence or devotion. Receiving Holy Communion often seemed routine. About ten years later, however, I was confronted with a different perspective out of nowhere.

I was struck with celiac disease — an allergic intolerance to gluten — and could no longer receive Holy Communion in the form of bread.[168] Fortunately for me, the Church is willing to accommodate this serious allergy by allowing people with celiac to receive Holy Communion under the species of wine, even if that is not

---

[168] In the Catholic Church, Holy Communion wafers must be made of wheat and contain gluten in order to be valid matter for consecration into the Body and Blood of Jesus.

being distributed to the congregation at Mass. With some adjustments, I am normally able to receive Holy Communion on Sundays in my home parish. This change, however, has meant that Holy Communion is no longer routine for me. Receiving now requires effort on my part and accommodations from others, especially if I am not attending Mass at my home parish. In this way, having celiac has been a blessing to me because I am now grateful for every Holy Communion.

I also recently learned the power of the Eucharist by experiencing its absence over an extended period of time. When the COVID pandemic and accompanying lockdowns took place in the spring of 2020, the churches were closed for fear of sickness. No one could receive Holy Communion for months. As the weeks passed by, I began to long more and more to receive Holy Communion. I could feel the strength and peace that was missing from my life.

Even once everyone else was allowed to start receiving Holy Communion under the form of bread, I was not allowed to receive the Precious Blood from a chalice for fear of spreading sickness. Finally, a courageous priest, upon hearing that I continued to be unable to receive, offered to consecrate a separate chalice for me. I was truly overjoyed to be able to receive the Precious Blood of Jesus again!

I pray that you would not have to lose access to the Eucharist in order to give it the importance it deserves in your life. There is power in the Blood!

The Scripture passage for this power tool comes from the book of the prophet Zechariah. In this quote, the prophet references the Blood of the covenant and encourages the "prisoners of hope" to return to their stronghold. Are you a prisoner of hope? Is the Eucharist your stronghold?

If we are in captivity, we must be a prisoner of hope! To be a prisoner of hope is to already have victory and freedom in sight. Freedom from the waterless pit — an empty and barren place. The Blood of the covenant is so powerful that we receive not only freedom but also restoration. What a mighty God we serve!

Many of us are lost in a spiritual Egypt, prisoners of our sins. Ruled by a foreign king with no mercy. We need to cover ourselves in the Precious Blood and be released from bondage. We can apply the blood of Jesus through our acceptance of him as our Saviour and we appropriate the Blood by faith.

> *The blood shall be a sign for you, upon the houses where you are; and when I see the blood, I will pass over you, and no plague shall fall upon you to destroy you, when I smite the land of Egypt. (Exodus 12:13, RSV-CE).*

After many signs and wonders in Egypt at the hand of Moses, Pharaoh would not relent and release the

Israelites from captivity. God therefore instructed the Israelites to mark the doorposts of their houses with the blood of the lamb. God promised that the destroyer would not enter their houses to kill them if they did so.

> *For the Lord will pass through to slay the Egyptians; and when he sees the blood on the lintel and on the two doorposts, the Lord will pass over the door, and will not allow the destroyer to enter your houses to slay you. (Ex. 12:23, RSV-CE).*

Once we are set free from captivity, however, we must return to our stronghold. Our stronghold must be a fortress of defense against our enemies. Who is that enemy? There is a destroyer on the loose today, roaming about seeking someone to devour.[169] This destroyer is the angel of the bottomless pit of hell!

> *They have as king over them the angel of the bottomless pit; his name in Hebrew is Abad'don, and in Greek he is called Apol'lyon.[170] (Revelation 9:11, RSC-CE).*

To protect ourselves from the destroyer, we need to cover ourselves with the Precious Blood of Jesus Christ.[171]

---

[169] 1 Peter 5:8.

[170] Or "destroyer."

[171] 1 Peter 1:18-19, RSV-CE ("precious blood of Christ").

*[T]hey overcame him*[172] *by the blood of the Lamb. (Revelation 12:11, Douay-Rheims).*

**There is power in prayer invoking the Blood of Jesus.** "Blood was the first appeal of earth to Heaven. 'The voice of thy brother's blood crieth to me from the earth' (Genesis IV, 10)."[173] How much more will God hear those covered with the blood that purchased our salvation? Approach Him with great confidence!

*Therefore, brethren, since we have confidence to enter the sanctuary by the blood of Jesus, by the new and living way which he opened for us through the curtain, that is, through his flesh, and since we have a great priest over the house of God, let us draw near with a true heart in full assurance of faith, with our hearts sprinkled clean from an evil conscience and our bodies washed with pure water. (Hebrews 10:19-22, RSV-CE).*

Battles have literally been won by invoking the Blood of Jesus. "St. Clare is said to have warded off the Saracens from scaling the walls of her convent by having recourse to the Precious Blood in the following prayer: 'We beseech

---

[172] The "accuser of our brethren," i.e., the devil.

[173] Walz, *Devotion to the Precious Blood,* at 7 (1926) (republished by Refuge of Sinners Publishing, Inc. 2013).

Thee, O Lord, help Thy servants whom Thou hast redeemed with Thy Precious Blood.'"[174]

Even Jesus is portrayed in Scripture as being sprinkled with the blood in Heaven:

> *And he was clothed with a garment sprinkled with blood; and his name is called, THE WORD OF GOD. (Revelation 19:13, Douay-Rheims).*

I cover you now in the Blood of Jesus! I apply the Blood of Jesus by faith to your body, soul and spirit. I cover your work, finances and sources of supply in the Blood of Jesus. I cover your coming and going in the Blood of Jesus. May you be healed and delivered from all bondage by the Precious Blood of Jesus Christ!

Amen!

---

[174] *Devotion to the Precious Blood*, at 222.

## Additional Resources

Related Scriptures:

Genesis 49:11; Isaiah 1:18; Dan. 12:1; Heb. 13:11-12; Rev. 7:13-17.

Songs:

*"There is Power in the Blood"* — Amy Grant (Music video by Amy Grant performing Power In The Blood (2015). (A YouTube video (with lyrics) of the song can be watched here: https://tinyurl.com/yy6yklhj.)

*"There is Power in the Blood"* — The Charlie Daniels Band from the Album *How Sweet the Sound: 25 Favorite Hymns and Gospel Greats* (2002).
(A YouTube video of the song can be watched here: https://tinyurl.com/y5zelsqw.)

Prayer:

> *O almighty and everlasting God, who didst appoint Thine only-begotten Son the Redeemer of the world, and hast willed to be appeased by His blood; grant unto us, we beseech Thee, so to venerate with solemn worship the price of our redemption, and by its power be so defended against the evils of this life, that we may enjoy the fruit thereof for evermore in heaven.*

*Collect* (Prayer) for the Feast of the Most Precious Blood of Our Lord Jesus Christ (July 1) (Roman Catholic Traditional Latin Mass (Extraordinary Form)).

Additional Reading:

Appendix 1, Litany of the Most Precious Blood of Our Lord Jesus Christ.

Additional Points for Reflection:

Journey to the Promised Land: Exodus 12:21-27.

Armor of God: Ephesians 2:13.

Beatitude: Matthew 5:7.

Gift of the Holy Spirit: Healing.

# The Power of Belief

## Promise in God's Word

*Put on the whole armor of God, that you may be able to stand against the wiles of the devil. . . . [A]bove all taking the shield of faith, with which you can quench all the flaming darts of the evil one. (Ephesians 6:11, 16, RSV-CE).*

## Reflection

Do you believe in Jesus? This is important. This is the over-arching shield in the armor of God. Stop for a minute and think about this question.

I am not talking about a mere belief in the historical Jesus. "It is possible to know and believe all these historical facts about Jesus and yet not be a Christian; because Christianity is not about the knowing and believing of facts alone; instead, it is the following of a person — the Man Jesus Christ."[175] Even non-Christians believe that a man named Jesus walked the earth; some even believe he was a prophet. I am also not talking about the modernist Jesus who is portrayed as just another "good man" while denying that He worked any miracles.

---

[175] Rev. Bro. Augustine Momoh, O.P., *Step Into the Flames and Rescue Souls*, at 19 (Newborne Enterprises) (1997).

Jesus said to St. Thomas, "Do not be faithless, but believing."[176] All things are possible to him who believes![177] What we need is saving faith.[178] We need expectant faith that God can and will work a miracle. We need to have more than just historical faith or intellectual faith. We need faith not feelings.

In 2003, I traveled to Nigeria for the first time to visit friends our family had met in the United States. The focus of the trip was to spend time with a Catholic prayer ministry run by a Dominican Brother and visit the Dominican community. I had recently recovered from an infection that had made me quite sick and had to take a batch of vaccines to travel to Africa. The yellow fever vaccine made me sick for several days. One of the first nights in Lagos, I participated in an all-night prayer vigil with the prayer team. I had never seen anything like it! Radical prayer of fire for hours.

As the night went on, however, I began to experience heaviness in my legs and fatigue set in. Over the following several days, I had difficulty sleeping, started to experience stress, anxiety and fear, and was generally not doing well. Things calmed down towards the end of the

---

[176] John 20:27, RSV-CE.

[177] Mark 9:23.

[178] *Step Into the Flames,* at 19-22.

trip as I rested and recovered. I returned to the United States and life continued as normal.

It was only years later, after working with the prayer ministry and learning about intercession, healing and deliverance prayer, that I came to understand my experience in Nigeria. What I realized is that, while the prayers said over me on my retreat in Omaha[179] had bound up and chained demonic influences to sin and addiction, I had not gone through deliverance at that time. There remained vestiges of the demonic influences, whether you call them spiritual infection, deposits, spiritual baggage, hooks, lines or tentacles. There may have still been open doors in the spirit to attacks by demonic entities or ancestral issues. On top of all that, there were the physical realities of having been through a difficult illness before the trip and the effects of jet lag.

Despite all the variables, I have concluded that participating in the night vigil and being exposed to serious fire of the Holy Spirit had confronted the residue of the enemy in my life and I had experienced negativity as a result. The anxiety and fear I experienced was not entirely me — the enemy was projecting those emotions on me because they were experiencing fear at the confrontation with the power of Almighty God. The physical discomfort I experienced was not entirely fatigue from having been sick and international travel — it was

---

[179] *See* the chapter on *The Power of Patience,* above.

also discomfort at the enemy's baggage in my spirit being destroyed by fire. Unfortunately, no one had explained any of this to me before the experience.

As the years passed and I was cleansed by the Holy Spirit and set free, I also learned that it can be difficult to distinguish self-deliverance and spiritual warfare from intercession for others. Those who are in Christ can be asked by God to intercede for others in the spirit *and* body. This experience can involve us having to carry and battle with the sins of the other person, to help win graces with Jesus for the other person to overcome and be set free. We may be confronted by unusual temptations. We must resist with God's grace in order to help the other person carry their cross in the spirit. We may also experience emotions that are unusual for us or out of context. The Lord may allow this burden to lead us to pray for those suffering from these emotions.[180]

The reality of spiritual warfare can be troubling to some. So why am I telling you about this? It is neither to cause fear over demonic influence nor to cause presumption about being a "suffering soul" for Christ. Rather, it is to *alleviate fear* and to *provide confidence in the Lord*.

---

[180] The exorcist Msgr. Stephen Rosetti makes reference to this phenomenon on his blog about his exorcism ministry. (http://tinyurl.com/2j6sbeue).

We must remain calm under all circumstances. Faith is our guide, not our feelings. My first experience in Nigeria with intense Holy Ghost fire produced unpleasant feelings, including fear. My faith and reason told me, however, that I was with faith-filled Christian ministers of the Gospel. I made a decision in my will to stay the course and, over the long-term, the Lord took care of the underlying issues that had caused me discomfort.

St. Paul understood "the immeasurable greatness of his power in us who believe"[181] and prayed for us to receive that revelation. If God is in us, can we not manifest His power now in our life? Indeed, Jesus told us that signs would accompany those who believe.[182]

Who is the Jesus we need to believe in to put on the shield of faith? We are talking about Jesus, the Son of the Living God, the Second Person of the Trinity, the Christ,[183] who

> *[f]or us men and for our salvation he came down from heaven, and by the Holy Spirit was incarnate of the Virgin Mary, and became man. For our sake he was crucified under Pontius Pilate, he suffered*

---

[181] Ephesians 1:18-19.

[182] Mark 16:16-18.

[183] "The word Christ, *Christos*, the Greek equivalent of the Hebrew Messias, means "anointed." Maas, A. (1910). Origin of the Name of Jesus Christ. In *The Catholic Encyclopedia*. New York: Robert Appleton Company. Retrieved August 8, 2020, from New Advent: http://tinyurl.com/3bek7z6t.

*death and was buried, and rose again on the third day in accordance with the Scriptures. He ascended into heaven and is seated at the right hand of the Father. He will come again in glory to judge the living and the dead and his kingdom will have no end.*[184]

I am talking about the Jesus who said:

*"All authority in heaven and on earth has been given to me." (Matthew 28:18, RSV-CE).*

This is the Jesus that we believe in. This Jesus is alive today and has been given all authority in heaven and on earth by God the Father.

Do you believe?

Do you believe that He loves you? Do you believe that He will act on your behalf? Do you believe that He will bring you peace?

Belief in Jesus is the foundation of Christianity. Christians are referred to as "believers" in the Bible.[185] "Being Christian is not the result of an ethical choice or a

---

[184] *Nicene Creed,* CCC Part I, Section 2.

[185] For example, *see* Acts 4:32, 5:14, 10:45; 2 Corinthians 6:15; 1 Thessalonians 1:7; 1 Timothy 5.

lofty idea, but the encounter with an event, a person, which gives life a new horizon and a decisive direction."[186]

We do not necessarily have to understand Jesus to be saved, but we need to believe in Him.[187] This saving faith makes us "obedient to Jesus and brings about a way of life that makes [us] different from the people of the world."[188]

The Bible tells us that belief in Jesus makes us a child of God:

> *Every one who believes that Jesus is the Christ is a child of God. (1 John 5:1, RSV-CE).*
>
> *[T]o all who received him, who believed in his name, he gave power to become children of God. (John 1:12, RSV-CE).*

In addition to belief, Jesus instructed his disciples to baptize all believers for salvation:[189]

> *He who believes and is baptized will be saved; but he who does not believe will be condemned. (Mark 16:16, RSV-CE).*

---

[186] *God is Love (Deus Caritas Est)*, Encyclical Letter of Benedict XVI, at 1 (Pauline Books & Media 2006).

[187] *Step Into the Flames*, at 19.

[188] *Id.* at 19-20.

[189] Baptism is necessary for salvation. CCC § 1257; Fanning, W. (1907). Baptism. In *The Catholic Encyclopedia*. New York: Robert Appleton Company. Retrieved August 8, 2020, from New Advent: http://tinyurl.com/3jh3x43y.

> *And Jesus came and said to them . . . "Go therefore and make disciples of all nations, baptizing them in the name of the Father and of the Son and of the Holy Spirit, teaching them to observe all that I have commanded you." (Matthew 28:18-20, RSV-CE).*

We see the requirement of belief in Christ prefigured in the Old Testament. Among the Israelites, those who did not believe were unable to enter the Promised Land.[190] Now, under the New Covenant, belief in Jesus is the key to eternal life. It is not an academic question. It is of eternal significance to you whether or not you believe in Jesus.

> *"Truly, truly, I say to you, he who believes has eternal life." (John 6:47, RSV-CE).*

> *Jesus said to her, "I am the resurrection and the life; he who believes in me, though he die, yet shall he live, and whoever lives and believes in me shall never die." (John 11:25-26, RSV-CE).*

> *For God so loved the world that he gave his only Son, that whoever believes in him should not perish but have eternal life. (John 3:16, RSV-CE).*

In all three of these passages above, the word "believe" comes from the same Greek word — *pisteuō*. This word appears over two hundred forty times in the New Testament! In the Latin Vulgate translation of the

---

[190] *See* Hebrews 3:19.

Bible, the Latin word used is "credo." This is how the Nicene Creed starts – "Credo in unum Deum."[191]

The Bible records many signs done by Jesus in the presence of the disciples after His resurrection from the dead. St. John tells us that they were "written that you may believe that Jesus is the Christ, the Son of God, and that believing you may have life in his name."[192] The same word for "believe" is again used here twice. Jesus also said, "Blessed are those who have not seen and yet believe."[193] This is the same word for "believe" here as well.

We see that belief in Jesus is important. And we see that the word for "believe" is used throughout the New Testament. So what does it mean to "believe" in Jesus? How do we access this power tool?

There is one story in the Bible that always comes to mind when I am confronting my lack of belief in Jesus in a specific moment.[194] A man had brought his son to Jesus for healing and deliverance — the child had a dumb spirit

---

[191] "I believe in one God." *Nicene Creed,* CCC Part I, Section 2. The Nicene Creed was adopted at the Council of Nicea in 325 and the Council of Constantinople in 381, and again confirmed in the Council of Chalcedon in 451. It has been recited every Sunday as part of the Catholic Mass since at least the 6th Century. *See* Appendix 2.

[192] John 20:31, RSV-CE.

[193] John 20:29, RSV-CE.

[194] Mark 9:14-29.

that would dash him to the ground, where he would foam and grind his teeth, becoming rigid. The man asked the disciples to cast it out, but they could not. Jesus responds, "O faithless generation, how long am I to be with you? How long am I to bear with you? Bring him to me." When the boy was brought to Jesus and the evil spirit saw Him, the boy fell on the ground and began manifesting. Jesus asked the father, "How long has he had this?" The father replied, "Since childhood . . . if you can do anything, have pity on us and help us." This is the key moment in the story:

> *And Jesus said to him, "If you can!* ***All things are possible to him who believes****." Immediately the father of the child cried out and said, "****I believe; help my unbelief!****" (Mark 9:23-24, RSV-CE) (emphasis added).*

At this expression of faith, Jesus rebuked the evil spirit and cast it out of the boy.

Jesus immediately confronted the weak belief of the father in this story who was seeking healing and deliverance for his son. His response, "If you can! All things are possible to him who believes," provoked not only a profession of belief from the father, but also a petition to Jesus to "help my unbelief!"

One very important lesson we learn from this is that it is necessary to manifest our belief in Jesus outwardly, even if our faith is weak. In fact, we strengthen our faith by making acts of faith! Making a daily Act of Faith is a traditional practice to help us grow in this area.

This is also a powerful prayer for us in times of wobbly belief. We can cry out to Jesus as well, "I believe; help my unbelief!" We should nevertheless take heart when we struggle to believe — even the disciples found themselves being chastised by Jesus after the resurrection for being slow to believe.[195]

Belief in Jesus is critical to obtaining what we are seeking in our prayers for ourselves. There are many examples in the Bible where healing is tied to belief in Jesus.[196] "Faith is manifested through obedience."[197] Many times, Jesus draws out a manifestation of belief before He works the miraculous healing on their behalf.[198]

Have you believed the word that Jesus has spoken to you? Be healed in the Name of Jesus!

---

[195] Luke 24:25.

[196] *See* Matthew 8:13, 9:28; Mark 5:36; Luke 8:50; John 4:50.

[197] *God's Armor*, at 39.

[198] *See, e.g.*, Matthew 12:13; Mark 3:5, 9:23-24; Luke 17:11-14; John 4:46-54. For an example in the Old Testament of the Prophet Elijah drawing out the faith of the widow before the miracle takes place, *see* 1 Kings 17:8-16 (RSV-CE).

There are many other promises in the Bible that also flow from belief in Jesus:

- You shall receive forgiveness of your sins in His name.[199]
- You shall receive salvation.[200]
- You shall not remain in darkness.[201]
- You shall never thirst spiritually.[202]
- You shall overcome the world.[203]

Jesus also prayed for those who would believe because of the word of the original disciples handed down over the generations. As one of his disciples, the prayer of Jesus applies to you![204]

In the Name of Jesus, I ask Almighty God to grant you the gift of saving faith in His Son Jesus Christ, that you will receive forgiveness of your sins and salvation in His Name. Amen!

---

199 Acts 10:43.

200 Mark 16:16; Acts 16:31.

201 John 12:46.

202 John 6:35, 7:38.

203 1 John 5:5.

204 John 17:15-23.

## Additional Resources

Related Scriptures:

Mark 11:24; Luke 8:12-13; John 1:7, 1:50, 2:11, 3:18, 3:36, 5:24, 6:40, 9:35-38, 14:1; Romans 4, 10:11; 1 John 3:23, 5:13.

Songs:

*"Credo V"* — Monastic Choir of the Abbey Notre Dame de Fontgombault from the album *The Assumption* (1997) (video released on Jan. 13, 2017).
(A YouTube video of the song can be watched here: https://tinyurl.com/y4jcfb7c.)

*"African Credo — I Believe"* — Song by Jude Nnam (video by Catholic Television of Nigeria).
(A YouTube video of the song can be watched here: https://tinyurl.com/y342z7xe.)

*"This I Believe (The Creed)"* — Song by Hillsong Worship recorded live at Hillsong Conference in Sydney (2014).
(A YouTube video of the song can be watched here: https://tinyurl.com/mjfpn4q.)

*"Believe"* — Song by Hillsong Worship from the album *Beautiful Exchange* (Released July 2010)
(A YouTube video of the song can be watched here: https://tinyurl.com/y6s5rmf9.)

Prayer:

Appendix 2, The Nicene Creed.

Traditional Act of Faith (Baltimore Catechism):

> *O my God! I firmly believe that Thou art one God in three Divine Persons, the Father, the Son, and the Holy Ghost;*
>
> *I believe that Thy Divine Son became man, and died for our sins, and that He will come to judge the living and the dead.*
>
> *I believe these and all the truths which the Holy Catholic Church teaches, because Thou hast revealed them, Who canst neither deceive nor be deceived. Amen.*

Additional Reading:

CCC Part I, Section 2, Chapter 2 ("I believe in Jesus Christ, the Only Son of God"), § 422 *et seq.*

Additional Points for Reflection:

Journey to the Promised Land: Num. 14:26-30.

Armor of God: Ephesians 6:16.

Beatitude: Matthew 5:11.

Gift of the Holy Spirit: Faith.

# The Power of the Name of Jesus

## Promise in God's Word

*All who call upon the name of the Lord shall be delivered. (Joel 2:32, RSV-CE).*[205]

## Reflection

The Scriptures tell us that "there is no other name under heaven given among men by which we must be saved."[206] Before His birth, Mary and Joseph were both given divine instruction about the naming of the divine child.

The angel Gabriel appeared to Mary, and announced to her:

> *And behold, you will conceive in your womb and bear a son, and you shall call his name Jesus. (Luke 1:31, RSV-CE).*

An angel also appeared to St. Joseph in a dream and instructed him on the name for his son:

> *[S]he will bear a son, and you shall call his name Jesus, for he will save his people from their sins. (Matthew1:21, RSV-CE).*

---

[205] *See also* Romans 10:13.

[206] Acts 4:12, RSV-CE.

St. Luke confirms for us that the Name of Jesus is of heavenly origin:

> *[A]t the end of eight days, when he was circumcised, he was called Jesus, the name given by the angel before he was conceived in the womb. (Luke 2:21, RSV-CE).*

The name Jesus means in Hebrew "God saves."[207] It is a name that expresses both His identity and His mission.[208]

Jesus saves! This is not just a catchy Christian slogan. It is the Truth. "[E]very one who believes in him receives forgiveness of sins through his name."[209] I pray that you would believe in The Name! Jesus is the Name above all other names.[210]

The Name of Jesus is a powerful offensive weapon in our prayers for ourselves. St. Paul tells us to "take . . . the sword of the Spirit, which is the word of God."[211] The Word of God is Jesus Himself.[212] By taking up the Name

---

207 CCC § 430.

208 *Id.*

209 Acts 10:43, RSV-CE.

210 Philippians 2:9-11; *see* Hebrews 1:4.

211 Ephesians 6:17, RSV-CE.

212 John 1:1, 14.

of Jesus in prayer, by believing in Him, we are wielding a powerful two-edged sword![213]

> *For the word of God is living and active, sharper than any two-edged sword, piercing to the division of soul and spirit, of joints and marrow, and discerning the thoughts and intentions of the heart. (Hebrews 4:12, RSV-CE).*

Standing firmly on this foundation of faith, belief in the Name of Jesus, miracles become possible in our lives. The first miracle recorded in the Acts of the Apostles focuses on the use of the Name of Jesus for a miraculous healing by St. Peter:

> *"I give you what I have; in the name of Jesus Christ of Nazareth, walk." (Acts 3:6, RSV-CE).*

St. Peter went on to explain the power of the Name to the crowd:

> *"And his name, by faith in his name, has made this man strong." (Acts 3:16, RSV-CE).*

It often seems that we miss the point of this story today, when we throw out the words "in the Name of Jesus" at the end of every prayer, as if uttering those words was all that was necessary to make God answer the prayer. We do not offer our prayers "in the Name of Jesus" as a mantra, or a talisman, that evokes something

---

[213] *See* Revelation 1:16.

by mere recital of the words. The sons of Sceva learned this the hard way.[214]

To act "in the name" of another is an official act on their behalf. If I appoint someone to act in my name, they are authorized to act as my agent. The agent can sign a contract on my behalf or take other official legal action "in my name." If someone is acting "in the name of the law," they are acting with the authority of the government.

When we pray in the Name of Jesus, we stand in the shoes of Jesus. We pray in His place. We are praying to the Father as Jesus. We place the mantle of Jesus over our shoulders.[215]

When the Father looks at us, does He see Jesus when we pray in His Name? When our prayer rises to the Father, does He hear Jesus when we pray in His Name? We must become like Jesus to pray to the Father in His Name.

The apostles had been transformed and made clean by the word Jesus had spoken to them while He was with them.[216] When Jesus ascended into Heaven, He sent the Holy Spirit to complete the work of transformation. The apostles were baptized with fire at Pentecost and were like new men. They assumed the mantle of Christ, the mantle

---

214 Acts 19:13-16.

215 *Compare* 1 Kings 19:19.

216 John 15:3.

of evangelism, to spread the gospel of salvation to the ends of the earth. And the Father began working miracles, signs and wonders to confirm the message, in the Name of His Son Jesus.[217]

The Gospel tells us that Jesus told the disciples that He would go to the Father, and the Father would send the Holy Spirit *in His Name.*[218] Thus, when we pray to the Father in the Name of Jesus, we pray that the Father would act in Jesus' Name, for the glory of Jesus and His Kingdom. We pray in Jesus' Name that the Father would *move in power.* That He would *send forth His Spirit.* Indeed, our entire life should be lived in the Name of Jesus:

> *And whatever you do, in word or deed, do everything in the name of the Lord Jesus, giving thanks to God the Father through him. (Colossians 3:17, RSV-CE).*

I pray that as you reflect and pray on the power tools in these books, that the Father sends the Holy Spirit upon you to transform you day by day more into the likeness of His Son Jesus, and that as you call upon His Name you will be healed and delivered.

---

217 Acts 4:29-30; *see also* Mark 16:17; Acts 2:22, 5:12, 14:3; Hebrews 2:4.

218 John 14:26.

## Additional Resources

Related Scriptures:

Luke 4:16-21; 1 John 3:23; Song 1:3; Isaiah 61:1.

Songs:

*"In Jesus' Name (feat. Michael W. Smith, Natalie Grant & Michael Tait)"* — Song by Third Day from the album *Lead Us Back: Songs of Worship* (Deluxe Edition) (2015).
(A YouTube video of the song can be watched here: https://tinyurl.com/y4e48rwn.)

*"What A Beautiful Name"* — Song by Hillsong Worship (2016).
(A YouTube video of the song can be watched here: https://tinyurl.com/y2mjxeqt.)

*"Love Has A Name"* — Song by Jesus Culture featuring Kim Walker-Smith from the album *Love Has A Name* (Released 2017).
(A YouTube video of the song can be watched here: https://tinyurl.com/y84zzujq.)

*"Resurrecting"* — Song by Elevation Worship from the album *Here As In Heaven* (Released 2016).
(A YouTube video of the live performance of the song can be watched here: https://tinyurl.com/35yn4hfn.)

*"His Name"* — Song by Urban Rescue from the album *Wild Heart* (Released 2016).
(A YouTube video of the song can be watched here: https://tinyurl.com/y3rb48ay.)

Prayer:

> *O God, who didst appoint Thine only-begotten Son to be the Saviour of mankind, and didst bid that He should be called Jesus; mercifully grant that we, who venerate His holy Name on earth, may also enjoy the vision of Him in heaven.*

*Collect* (Prayer) for the Feast of the Holy Name of Jesus (Roman Catholic Traditional Latin Mass (Extraordinary Form)).

Appendix 3, Litany of the Most Holy Name of Jesus.

Additional Reading:

Fr. Paul O'Sullivan, O.P., *The Wonders of the Holy Name* (originally published in 1946) (TAN Books 1993).

Additional Points for Reflection:

Journey to the Promised Land: Exodus 17:1-7; 1 Cor. 10:4.

Armor of God: Ephesians 6:17.

Beatitude: *See* John 3:16-18.

Gift of the Holy Spirit: Miracles.

# The Power of Fire

## Promise in God's Word

*Is not my word like fire, says the Lord, and like a hammer which breaks the rock in pieces? (Jeremiah 23:29, RSV-CE).*

## Reflection

I believe in the fire of the Holy Spirit! "We need the fire of the Holy Spirit to be able to counter powers of spiritual wickedness."[219] If you have not encountered the fire of the Holy Spirit in your prayer life, ask the Holy Spirit to send the fire now!

My first encounter with fire evangelism was in the basement chapel of a Catholic Church in Washington, D.C. We had been invited to a healing service by a friend. The service was being led by a Dominican brother from Nigeria. After preaching, Brother Augustine prayed over the crowd. People then came up for individual prayer.

Brother prayed over someone and released the fire of the Holy Spirit. "Fire!" The person fell to the ground and began moving like a snake. Although I was familiar with people resting in the Spirit from charismatic services, this was different. Several other people exhibited

---

[219] Rev. Fr. Kingsley Okbuji, SSJ, *Praying Aggressively to Counter Spiritual Wickedness!*, at 30 (Christian Faith Publishing, Inc. 2020).

manifestations during the prayers of fire. It occurred to me that these manifestations of demonic influence when encountering the Holy Spirit were biblical.

The fire of God is not just an image, it is a reality. The Bible teaches that God makes his servants flames of fire.[220] Are you on fire for God yet?

The Scriptures describe God as a consuming fire.[221] "God is a raging fire of love and holiness, which is warming and purifying to the saints but searing and punishing to the sinner."[222] Thus, when God appears to Moses in the burning bush, "the bush was burning, yet it was not consumed."[223]

God manifested Himself to the Israelites in the desert as a pillar of fire, leading their way in the dark of night.[224] "If we be vigilant, we too have a pillar of fire, the grace of the spirit."[225]

The Holy Spirit famously appears as tongues of fire falling on the apostles at Pentecost.[226] The Holy Spirit is

---

220 Hebrews 1:7; *see also* Sirach 48:1; Ps. 104:4.

221 Hebrews 12:29.

222 *Ignatius Catholic Study Bible New Testament*, note at Hebrews 12:29, at 435 (citing Deut. 4:24).

223 Exodus 3:2.

224 Exodus 13:21.

225 *St. John Chysostom on Ephesians*, Chapter 6, *supra.*

226 Acts 2:3.

also called the flame of love. "This flame of love is the Spirit of its Bridegroom, who is the Holy Spirit."[227]

There are several times in the Old Testament when the fire of God falls from heaven and manifests in the physical world. Fire came down from heaven to consume the sacrifice that David offered on the threshing floor of Ornan the Jebusite.[228] Fire fell to consume the sacrifice at the dedication of the temple, in the presence of King Solomon and the people of Israel.[229] "[T]he Lord rained on Sodom and Gomor'rah brimstone and fire from the Lord out of heaven" due to their sins.[230] Fire came from the rock to consume the offering of Gideon to confirm his calling.[231]

One of my favorite stories in the Bible involves Elijah challenging the prophets of the pagan god Baal to a "prayer duel." At the direction of the Lord, Elijah sought out the King of Israel, Ahab. Elijah confronted Ahab that he had abandoned the commandments of God and instead followed false gods. He told Ahab to "gather all Israel to me at Mount Carmel, and the four hundred and fifty

---

227 *The Collected Words of St. John of the Cross,* at 641 (ICS Publications 1991).

228 1 Chronicles 21:26, RSV-CE.

229 2 Chronicles 7:1.

230 Genesis 19:24, RSV-CE.

231 Judges 6:21.

prophets of Ba'al and the four hundred prophets of Ashe'rah, who eat at Jez'ebel's table."[232]

Ahab did as requested, and everyone gathered at Mount Carmel. Elijah first challenged the people of Israel, "How long will you go limping with two different opinions? If the Lord is God, follow him; but if Ba'al, then follow him."[233]

Receiving no answer, Elijah turned to the four hundred fifty prophets of Baal and challenged them to a duel. Each side would prepare a bull for sacrifice on wood but not light the wood on fire. Each would then call on their god, and "the God who answers by fire, he is God."[234]

The prophets of Baal accepted the challenge and prepared the altar. They cried out all morning, but no one answered. "And at noon Elijah mocked them, saying, 'Cry aloud, for he is a god; either he is musing, or he has gone aside, or he is on a journey, or perhaps he is asleep and must be awakened.'"[235] The crazed prophets of Baal continued their cries to their god, cutting themselves until blood gushed out, but there was still no voice.

It was Elijah's turn. He prepared the altar, but went on to have the people pour jars of water on the wood *three*

---

[232] 1 Kings 18:19, RSV-CE.

[233] 1 Kings 18:21, RSV-CE.

[234] 1 Kings 18:24, RSV-CE.

[235] 1 Kings 18:27, RSV-CE.

*times*, until water flowed around the altar and in a trench he dug around it. Elijah then prayed:

> *"O Lord, God of Abraham, Isaac, and Israel, let it be known this day that thou art God in Israel, and that I am thy servant, and that I have done all these things at thy word. Answer me, O Lord, answer me, that this people may know that thou, O Lord, art God, and that thou hast turned their hearts back." (1 Kings 18:36-37, RSV-CE).*

After his prayer, "the fire of the Lord fell, and consumed the burnt offering, and the wood, and the stones, and the dust, and licked up the water that was in the trench."[236] The people of Israel saw who was God! He did not let Elijah down![237]

We also learn that the prophet Elijah called down fire from heaven three times.[238] Elijah was a great warrior for God. Ask the Holy Spirit to reveal to you how this story is relevant to your battle.

I would not suggest engaging in this challenge without the prophetic anointing of Elijah resting upon you. "You shall not put the Lord your God to the test."[239]

---

[236] 1 Kings 18:38, RSV-CE.

[237] "This event was a 'figure' of the fire of the Holy Spirit, who transforms what he touches." (CCC § 696).

[238] 1 Kings 18:38; 2 Kings 1:10 and 12; *see also* Sirach 48:3.

[239] Deut. 6:16, RSV-CE; *see also* Matthew 4:7.

I do believe, however, that our God does answer by fire *in the spirit* for those who believe.

Not long after my first encounter with fire evangelism in Washington, D.C., we moved to Minnesota. During our two years in Minnesota, I participated in the Jesus Heals Ministry. Once a week, I would join prayer teams at a local convent for private prayer sessions with people seeking physical or spiritual healing.

It was during a prayer session at Jesus Heals Ministry that my belief in the reality of spiritual fire was strengthened. There were three of us praying on a team for one person. The initial discussion suggested that this person had some spiritual problems that needed prayers.

As we started, I was standing in the back praying silently while the team leader was praying out loud. The person was sitting in a chair with eyes closed and was not reacting to the prayers. We had been praying for a little while when something the leader prayed prompted me in the spirit to start praying "Holy Ghost fire" over and over again for this person. After about thirty seconds of fire prayers, she began crying out, "I see fire! There is fire everywhere!" The entire atmosphere of the prayer ministry had shifted as the Holy Spirit sent His fire. I believe in the fire of the Holy Spirit!

St. Paul teaches us that "we are not contending against flesh and blood, but against the principalities, against the powers, against the world rulers of this present darkness, against the spiritual hosts of wickedness in the heavenly places."[240] This is a spiritual battle, and we need spiritual weapons. This power tool teaches us that the Word of God itself is like fire. When we use the Scriptures as prayer points against the spiritual obstacles in our lives, the fire of God moves!

We can also pray aggressively with the fire of the Holy Spirit against the spiritual enemies that come against us.[241] We can pray that God will send His fire to consume our *spiritual* enemies, namely the devil and his demons.[242] Isaiah prayed, "Let the fire for thy adversaries consume them."[243] The Douay-Rheims translation of his prayer is even more dramatic, "Let fire devour thy enemies."[244] The psalmist also prays prophetically that the fire of God will consume His enemies:

> *Your hand will find out all your enemies; your right hand will find out those who hate you. You will make them as a blazing oven when you appear. The Lord will swallow them up in his wrath; and fire will consume them. (Psalm 21:8-9, RSV-CE).*

---

240 Ephesians 6:12, RSV-CE.

241 *See* Rev. Bro. Augustine Momoh, O.P., *Release Me, O Lord Jesus.*

242 Our Blessed Lord teaches us to love and pray for our *human* enemies. Matthew 5:43-48.

243 Isaiah 26:11, RSV-CE.

244 Isaiah 26:11, Douay-Rheims.

We need the fire of the Holy Spirit in our lives. Jesus longed to baptize the world with the fire of the Holy Spirit.[245] He cried out:

> *"I came to cast fire upon the earth; and would that it were already kindled! (Luke 12:49, RSV-CE).*

Pray right now that Jesus would send the fire of the Holy Spirit into your life! Holy Ghost fire! Holy Ghost fire! Holy Ghost fire! Holy Ghost fire! In the Name of Jesus, receive it now!

---

[245] Matthew 3:11 (*"he will baptize you with the Holy Spirit and with fire"*); Luke 3:16 (*"he will baptize you with the Holy Spirit and with fire"*); *see* John 1:33 (*"this is he who baptizes with the Holy Spirit"*); Mark 1:8 (*"he will baptize you with the Holy Spirit"*); Acts 19:1-6; *see also* Acts 1:5 (*"before many days you shall be baptized with the Holy Spirit"*).

## Additional Resources

Related Scriptures:

Exodus 14:24; Ps. 29:7, 97:1-5, 106:16-18, 140:9-10; Sir. 11:32; Lam. 1:13; Dan. 7:9-10; Isaiah 10:17, 47:14, 66:15-16; Mal. 3:1-3; Zech. 2:5; Ezek. 20:47-48; Mark 9:49; Acts 2:3-4; 2 Tim. 1:6-7.

Songs:

*"Set Me Ablaze"* — Song by Jesus Culture featuring Katie Torwalt from the album *Let It Echo* (Released 2015).
(A YouTube video of the acoustic version of the song can be watched here: https://tinyurl.com/y3mrrf4e.)

*"Let the Fire Fall"* — Song by John Michael Talbot from the album *Come Worship the Lord,* Vol. 1 (Released 1990).
(A YouTube video of the song can be watched here: https://tinyurl.com/dvctm6yw.)

*"Soul on Fire"* – Song by Third Day from the album *Lead Us Back* (Released 2014).
(A YouTube video of the song can be watched here: http://tinyurl.com/y2n28vsu.)

<u>Prayer:</u>

Veni, Sancte Spiritus:[246]

> *Come, Holy Spirit, fill the hearts of Thy faithful and kindle in them the fire of Thy love.*
>
> *V. Send forth Thy Spirit and they shall be created.*
>
> *R. And Thou shalt renew the face of the earth.*
>
> *Let us pray:*
>
> *O God, Who taught the hearts of the faithful by the light of the Holy Spirit, grant that, by the gift of the same Spirit, we may be always truly wise, and ever rejoice in His consolation. Through Christ our Lord.*
>
> *Amen.*

<u>Additional Reading:</u>

CCC § 696.

<u>Additional Points for Reflection:</u>

Journey to the Promised Land: Exodus 13:21.

Armor of God: Ephesians 6:18.

Beatitude: *See* Latt. 3:11; Luke 3:16.

Gift of the Holy Spirit: Holy Ghost Fire.

---

[246] The texts that compose this traditional private prayer of devotion to the Holy Spirit appear in the propers for the Feast of Pentecost in both the Traditional Latin Mass and Divine Office, and also in the votive Mass of the Holy Spirit.

# The Power of Mary

## Promise in God's Word

*The Lord hath blessed thee by his power, because by thee he hath brought our enemies to nought. . . . Blessed art thou, O daughter, by the Lord the most high God, above all women upon the earth. Blessed be the Lord who made heaven and earth, who hath directed thee to the cutting off the head of the prince of our enemies. (Judith 13:22-24, Douay-Rheims).*

## Reflection

We have been exploring various power tools in this book to support our prayers for ourselves. The Mother of Jesus is a powerful advocate for us with her Son. I personally experienced this intercession when I had been away from God for years.

I am a "cradle Catholic" and faithfully attended Mass every Sunday until I left for college and abandoned the Faith. Although I was married in the Catholic Church, my apostasy continued several years into my marriage. One day, my wife came home with a pile of books for a television show she was working on. The books were all about "Marian apparitions."[247] I had never heard of such

[247] A Marian apparition is a reported supernatural appearance by Mary, the mother of Jesus.

a thing. Curious, I picked up a book called "Fatima: The Great Sign"[248] on Our Lady of Fatima.[249] I finished reading the book that evening. As I put the book down, I told my wife, "I am going to hell." The next weekend I returned to the Church and have, by the grace of God, been faithful ever since.

I tell this story as a testimony to the power of Mary's intercession. I believe that as the result of my grandmother Mary having prayed the Rosary daily, the Mother of Jesus obtained from her Son the grace for my conversion, repentance and return to the Faith, for which I am eternally grateful. I cannot describe in words how the scales fell from my eyes that evening and I saw very clearly that were I to die and go to judgment that day I would be condemned to hell for my sins.

The Scriptures confirm the intercessory power of the Mother of Jesus.[250] We see the power of Mary's intercession from Jesus' first public miracle. Jesus was

---

[248] Francis Johnston, *Fatima: The Great Sign* (Tan Books & Publishers, Inc.) (1980).

[249] Mary appeared to three children in Fatima, Portugal in 1917. The apparitions culminated in the miracle of the sun, which was even documented by secular newspapers hostile to the Catholic Church.

[250] Despite modern hostility to Mary, the early Protestant reformers, including Luther, Zwingli and Calvin, expressed devotion to Mary. I can only encourage those of my brothers and sisters in Christ who may be wary of this chapter to read it prayerfully, asking the Holy Spirit for light and truth.

invited to a wedding at Cana in Galilee, and his mother was there.[251] It was brought to Mary's attention that the wine was running out. She told Jesus, "They have no wine."[252] Jesus responded mystically to her, "O woman, what have you to do with me? My hour has not yet come." Though this response may seem cryptic to us, she understood His meaning and said to the servants, "Do whatever he tells you."

Jesus told the servants to fill six stone jars with water, each holding twenty or thirty gallons, to draw some out and to take it to the steward. The steward tasted the wine, and told the bridegroom, "Every man serves the good wine first; and when men have drunk freely, then the poor wine; but you have kept the good wine until now."[253] Thus, Jesus worked His first public miracle at the request of His mother.

We also learn from Scripture that Jesus gave Mary to us as our spiritual mother. Those of us who keep the commandments of God and bear testimony to Jesus are her offspring:

---

[251] John 2:1-11.

[252] "Mary said to Jesus: *They have no Wine.* It is the office of the Mother of God to tell him of the wants of men, for she is also their Mother." Dom Guéranger, OSB, Vol. 3 *The Liturgical Year,* at 241 (Second Sunday after Epiphany) (1949) (Republished by St. Bonaventure Publications 2000).

[253] John 2:10, RSV-CE.

> *[T]he dragon was angry with the woman,[254] and went off to make war on the rest of her offspring, on those who keep the commandments of God and bear testimony to Jesus. (Revelation 12:17, RSV-CE).*

If you want to obtain the victory in spiritual warfare against the devil, ask Mary for help. "We know that all the power of the mother of God[255] is derived from the merits of her Son."[256] In the prophetic words of Mardochai in the Old Testament, we can cry out to Mary, "Speak to the king for us, and deliver us from death."[257]

Catholic exorcists, who battle the devil and his demons daily in their ministry, testify to the overpowering fear and hatred in the demons when Mary is invoked.[258] "Those of us in the combat zone and in the front line battle against the enemies and his foes, the help of our mother Mary is important when the battle is tense and all spiritual experience and human knowledge prove to no avail to

---

[254] The Revised Standard footnote here reads: "Mary, the mother of the Messiah, must also be included in the meaning."

[255] The title "Mother of God," denied by Nestorius, was vindicated to her by the General Council of Ephesus, in 431. "The mother of our race [Eve] brought punishment into the world, but the Mother of our Lord brought salvation into the world." St. Augustine, Sermon 18 on the Saints (*Brevarium Romanum,* 2d Nocturn at Matins, Sept. 8, Feast of Nativity of the Blessed Virgin Mary).

[256] *Haydock Bible,* at 17, footnote on Genesis 3:15.

[257] Esther 15:3, Douay-Rheims.

[258] *Deliverance Prayers,* at 9.

repatriate the enemy. Calling and invoking her name in faith is hellish to demons. In my experience words are not enough to express her maternal protection over those in the combat zone and in the front line battles."[259] Another says, "In my experience – so far I have performed 2,300 rites of exorcism – I can say that the invocation of the Most Holy Virgin Mary often provokes significant reactions in the person being exorcized."[260]

We also see in Scripture the role that Mary is to play in the spiritual war against the devil. Jesus referred to his mother as "Woman" at the wedding at Cana, alluding to the promise to the woman after the fall of mankind in the Garden of Eden:

> *I will put enmities between thee and the woman, and thy seed and her seed: she shall crush thy head, and thou shalt lie in wait for her heel. (Genesis 3:15, Douay-Rheims).*

The biblical text for this power tool comes from the Book of Judith.[261] Judith has been viewed as a type or

---

[259] Rev. Bro. Augustine Momoh, O.P., *Christian Faith and Supernatural Reality*, at 60 (Wellness for Humanity Ministry 2018).

[260] *Why the Devil Hates Mary*, CNA March 8, 2018 (quoting Italian exorcist) (available online as of Aug. 18, 2020, here: http://tinyurl.com/y6bbtzhm).

[261] Judith 13:22-24, Douay-Rheims. The Douay-Rheims translation of the Latin Vulgate Bible has these verses, while the Revised Standard Version is translated from the Greek Septuagint and does not contain these verses. St. Jerome's translation of Judith was directly from the Aramaic.

figure of Mary,[262] foreshadowing her role in crushing the head of Satan.

The Book of Judith tells the story of a siege of a city in Israel by the feared general of the Assyrian army, Holofernes. The courage of the people of Israel failed because they were surrounded and had no way of escape. The people begged their leaders to seek peace with the Assyrians in the hope they would not be massacred. The leaders agreed that if God did not deliver them in five days, they would surrender.

Judith, a wealthy widow who lived a life of prayer and fasting, confronted the leaders for putting God to the test like this. After a stirring prayer to Almighty God for assistance, Judith set out into the enemy's camp with her servant. Holofernes, captivated by Judith's beauty, admitted her into his presence. Several nights later, at a banquet, he drank too much wine and fell asleep. Left alone with him, Judith drew his sword and cut off his head. She left the camp with the head in her basket.

The next day, the Israelites hung the head of Holofernes from the wall of the city. When the Assyrians

---

[262] *Compare* Judith 13:22-24 *with* Luke 1:38 ("And the angel being come in, said unto her: Hail, full of grace, the Lord is with thee: blessed art thou among women.") and 1:48 ("for behold from henceforth all generations shall call me blessed.") (Douay-Rheims). Several statements about Judith, including the passage above, are applied to Mary in the liturgy of the Church. *See, for example, Breviarium Romanum, Assumption of Mary* at Lauds, Short Chapter.

found his headless body, they fell into confusion and fled. The army of Israel pursued them and obtained deliverance from the Assyrian army.

The Book of Judith concludes with a canticle of praise for Almighty God by Judith. She proclaims that, "The Lord Almighty has foiled them by the hand of a woman."[263] The vast army of Assyria, whose leader boasted that he would destroy Israel, defeated by the hand of a woman.

The devil cried out in his satanic pride, "I will ascend to heaven; above the stars of God I will set my throne on high."[264] Will the Mother of Jesus likewise play a role in crushing his proud head? My experience is yes, she will.

We started this book by looking at the power tool of truth. If you made a commitment to the truth, then ask Jesus to show you the truth about His mother. I pray now to our Heavenly Father that He would answer your prayer and show you the truth about the intercessory power of Mary, through the power of anointing of the Holy Spirit, in Jesus' Name! Amen.

---

[263] Judith 16:6 (RSV-CE).

[264] Isaiah 14:12-15.

## Additional Resources

Related Scriptures:

Judith 15:9-11; Song of Sol. 6:4; 1 Kings 2:19-20; Judg. 5:24-27; Luke 1:42-45, 46-55, 2:34-35; John 19:25-27.

Douay-Rheims: Canticle 6:3 ("Thou art beautiful, O my love, sweet and comely as Jerusalem: terrible as an army set in array.").

Songs:

*"Ave Maria"* — Song by Franz Schubert, sung by Luciano Pavarotti (Live at Dodger Stadium, Los Angeles, 1994). (A YouTube video of the song can be watched here: https://tinyurl.com/sulf448.)

*"Holy Mother"* — Song by Eric Clapton from the album *Pavarotti & Friends for War Child* (Released 1996). (A YouTube video of the song featuring Luciano Pavarotti and the East London Gospel Choir can be watched here: https://tinyurl.com/y2q4575v.)

Quotation:

> *"Her virginity and generosity in embracing heroic martyrdom has rendered her so agreeable to God that He will never refuse anything that she asks for us."*
>
> St. John Vianney.

Prayer:

*O God, who by the fruitful virginity of blessed Mary hast bestowed upon the human race the rewards of eternal salvation: grant, we beseech Thee, that we may experience the intercession of her, through whom we have been made worthy to receive the author of life, Jesus Christ Thy Son, our Lord : Who with Thee liveth and reigneth.*

*Collect* (Prayer) for the Circumcision of Our Lord and the Octave of the Nativity (January 1) (Roman Catholic Traditional Latin Mass (Extraordinary Form)).

Additional Prayer:

Rosary, Fourth Glorious Mystery — The Assumption of Mary (*see Ps. 45*) (Fruit of the mystery: devotion to Mary).

Hail Mary:[265]

*Hail Mary, full of grace, the Lord is with thee. Blessed art thou amongst women, and blessed is the fruit of thy womb, Jesus.*

*Holy Mary, Mother of God, pray for us sinners, now and at the hour of our death. Amen.*

---

[265] "During an exorcism," Father Gabriele Amorth (at the time the chief exorcist for the Diocese of Rome) remembers, "Satan told me, through the possessed person, 'Every Hail Mary of the Rosary is a blow to the head for me; if Christians knew the power of the Rosary, it would be the end of me!'"

Additional Reading:

Fulton Sheen, *The World's First Love: Mary, Mother of God* (originally published by McGraw-Hill Book Co., NY (1952) (new edition available at www.ignatius.com).

Additional Points for Reflection:

Journey to the Promised Land: Exodus 40:34; John 16:20.

Armor of God: Luke 2:35.

Beatitude: Matthew 5:5.

Gift of the Holy Spirit: Prophecy.

# Appendix I

## Litany of the Most Precious Blood of Our Lord Jesus Christ[266]

Lord, have mercy. *Lord, have mercy.*

Christ, have mercy. *Christ, have mercy.*

Lord, have mercy. *Lord, have mercy.*

Christ, hear us. *Christ, hear us.*

Christ, graciously hear us. *Christ, graciously hear us.*

God the Father of Heaven, *have mercy on us.*

God the Son, Redeemer of the world, *have mercy on us.*

God, the Holy Spirit, *have mercy on us.*

Holy Trinity, One God, *have mercy on us.*

Blood of Christ, only-begotten Son of the eternal Father, *save us.*

Blood of Christ, Incarnate Word or God, *save us.*

Blood of Christ, of the New and Eternal Testament, *save us.*

---

266 This Litany in honor of Jesus in His Most Precious Blood was drawn up by the Sacred Congregation of Rites and promulgated by Pope John XXIII on February 24, 1960.

Blood of Christ, falling upon the earth in Agony, *save us.*

Blood of Christ, shed profusely in the Scourging, *save us.*

Blood of Christ, flowing forth in the Crowning with Thorns, *save us.*

Blood of Christ, poured out on the Cross, *save us.*

Blood of Christ, price of our salvation, *save us.*

Blood of Christ, without which there is no forgiveness, *save us.*

Blood of Christ, Eucharistic drink and refreshment of souls, *save us.*

Blood of Christ, stream of mercy, *save us.*

Blood of Christ, victor over demons, *save us.*

Blood of Christ, courage of Martyrs, *save us.*

Blood of Christ, strength of Confessors, *save us.*

Blood of Christ, bringing forth Virgins, *save us.*

Blood of Christ, help of those in peril, *save us.*

Blood of Christ, relief of the burdened, *save us.*

Blood of Christ, solace in sorrow, *save us.*

Blood of Christ, hope of the penitent, *save us.*

Blood of Christ, consolation of the dying, *save us.*

Blood of Christ, peace and tenderness of hearts, *save us.*

Blood of Christ, pledge of eternal life, *save us.*

Blood of Christ, freeing souls from purgatory, *save us.*

Blood of Christ, most worthy of all glory and honor, *save us.*

Lamb of God, who taketh away the sins of the world, *spare us, O Lord.*

Lamb of God, who taketh away the sins of the world, *graciously hear us, O Lord.*

Lamb of God, who taketh away the sins of the world, *have mercy on us, O Lord.*

V. Thou hast redeemed us, O Lord, in Thy Blood.

R. *And made us, for our God, a kingdom.*

Let us pray;

Almighty and eternal God, Thou hast appointed Thine only-begotten Son the Redeemer of the world and willed to be appeased by his blood. Grant, we beg of Thee, that we may worthily adore this price of our salvation and through its power be safeguarded from the evils of the present life so that we may rejoice in its fruits forever in heaven. Through the same Christ our Lord.

Amen.

# Appendix 2

## The Nicene Creed

I believe in one God, the Father almighty, maker of heaven and earth, of all things visible and invisible.

I believe in one Lord Jesus Christ, the Only Begotten Son of God, born of the Father before all ages.

God from God, Light from Light, true God from true God, begotten, not made, consubstantial with the Father; through him all things were made.

For us men and for our salvation he came down from heaven, and by the Holy Spirit was incarnate of the Virgin Mary, and became man.

For our sake he was crucified under Pontius Pilate, he suffered death and was buried, and rose again on the third day in accordance with the Scriptures.

He ascended into heaven and is seated at the right hand of the Father.

He will come again in glory to judge the living and the dead and his kingdom will have no end.

I believe in the Holy Spirit, the Lord, the giver of life, who proceeds from the Father and the Son, who with the Father and the Son is adored and glorified, who has spoken through the prophets.

I believe in one, holy, catholic and apostolic Church.

I confess one Baptism for the forgiveness of sins and I look forward to the resurrection of the dead and the life of the world to come.

Amen.[267]

---

[267] CCC Part I, Section 2 ("The Credo").

# Appendix 3

## Litany of the Most Holy Name of Jesus[268]

Lord, have mercy on us.

Christ, have mercy on us.

Lord, have mercy on us.

Jesus, hear us. *Jesus, graciously hear us.*

God, the Father of Heaven, *have mercy on us.*

God the Son, Redeemer of the world, *have mercy on us.*

God, the Holy Ghost, *have mercy on us.*

Holy Trinity, one God, *have mercy on us.*

Jesus, Son of the living God, *have mercy on us.*

Jesus, splendor of the Father, *have mercy on us.*

Jesus, brightness of eternal light, *have mercy on us.*

Jesus, King of glory, *have mercy on us.*

Jesus, sun of justice, *have mercy on us.*

Jesus, Son of the Virgin Mary, *have mercy on us.*

Jesus, most amiable, *have mercy on us.*

Jesus, most admirable, *have mercy on us.*

---

268 *The Raccolta*, at 53 (Benzinger Bros. 1957).

Jesus, the mighty God, *have mercy on us.*

Jesus, father of the world to come, *have mercy on us.*

Jesus, Angel of great counsel, *have mercy on us.*

Jesus, most powerful, *have mercy on us.*

Jesus, most patient, *have mercy on us.*

Jesus, most obedient, *have mercy on us.*

Jesus, meek and humble of heart, *have mercy on us.*

Jesus, lover of chastity, *have mercy on us.*

Jesus, lover of us, *have mercy on us.*

Jesus, God of peace, *have mercy on us.*

Jesus, author of life, *have mercy on us.*

Jesus, example of virtues, *have mercy on us.*

Jesus, zealous lover of souls, *have mercy on us.*

Jesus, our God, *have mercy on us.*

Jesus, our refuge, *have mercy on us.*

Jesus, father of the poor, *have mercy on us.*

Jesus, treasure of the faithful, *have mercy on us.*

Jesus, good Shepherd, *have mercy on us.*

Jesus, true light, *have mercy on us.*

Jesus, eternal wisdom, *have mercy on us.*

Jesus, infinite goodness, *have mercy on us.*

Jesus, our way and our life, *have mercy on us.*

Jesus, joy of angels, *have mercy on us.*

Jesus, King of Patriarchs, *have mercy on us.*

Jesus, Master of the Apostles, *have mercy on us.*

Jesus, Teacher of the Evangelists, *have mercy on us.*

Jesus, strength of Martyrs, *have mercy on us.*

Jesus, light of Confessors, *have mercy on us.*

Jesus, purity of Virgins, *have mercy on us.*

Jesus, crown of all Saints, *have mercy on us.*

Be merciful, *spare us, O Jesus!*

Be merciful, *graciously hear us, O Jesus!*

From all evil, *deliver us, O Jesus.*

From all sin, *deliver us, O Jesus.*

From Thy wrath, *deliver us, O Jesus.*

From the snares of the devil, *deliver us, O Jesus.*

From the spirit of fornication, *deliver us, O Jesus.*

From everlasting death, *deliver us, O Jesus.*

From the neglect of Thine inspirations, *deliver us, O Jesus.*

By the mystery of Thy holy Incarnation, *deliver us, O Jesus.*

By Thy Nativity, *deliver us, O Jesus.*

By Thine Infancy, *deliver us, O Jesus.*

By Thy most divine life, *deliver us, O Jesus.*

By Thy labors, *deliver us, O Jesus.*

By Thine agony and Passion, *deliver us, O Jesus.*

By Thy Cross and dereliction, *deliver us, O Jesus.*

By Thy Sufferings, *deliver us, O Jesus.*

By Thy death and burial, *deliver us, O Jesus.*

By Thy Resurrection, *deliver us, O Jesus.*

By Thine Ascension, *deliver us, O Jesus.*

By Thine institution of the most Holy Eucharist, *deliver us, O Jesus.*

By Thy joys, *deliver us, O Jesus.*

By Thy glory, *deliver us, O Jesus.*

Lamb of God, Who takest away the sins of the world, *spare us, O Jesus!*

Lamb of God, Who takest away the sins of the world, *hear us, O Jesus!*

Lamb of God, Who takest away the sins of the world, *have mercy on us, O Jesus!*

Jesus, hear us. *Jesus, graciously hear us.*

Let Us Pray.

O Lord Jesus Christ, who hast said, Ask and ye shall receive; seek, and ye shall find; knock, and it shall be opened unto you; mercifully attend to our supplications, and grant us the gift of Thy divine charity, that we may ever love Thee with our whole heart, and with all our words and deeds, and may never cease from praising Thee.

Make us, O Lord, to have a perpetual fear and love of Thy Holy Name, for Thou never failest to help and govern those whom Thou dost bring up in Thy steadfast love: who livest and reignest for ever and ever.

Amen.